I0157185

A Fat Man at War

Prose, Poetry, and Fragments

by

Tim Connelly

Copyright@2007 by Tim Connelly

All rights reserved. No part of this book may be reproduced in any manner without written consent except for the quotation of short passages used inside of an article, criticism. or review.

ISBN: 9780-6151-8582-8

A Fat Man At War

I weighed 210 pounds when I joined the Army after graduating high school. I went to basic training and was always a target for the drill instructors. I was different. I was the one who would cause problems in combat. At the start of basic, I failed the PT test. If a person didn't score at least 350 on the test, they had to repeat basic training in the "fat guy" platoon. I had no intention of going through basic twice. I lost 25 pounds and passed the PT test and went home on leave a lean, somewhat mean, fighting machine. I was sent to Germany to fight the Cold War. I weighted 175 pounds when I got to Germany. 18 months later, I tipped the scales at 250 pounds. It was the beer and snitzels that I had consumed to defeat the boredom of fighting Communism. I figured I could get out of going to war because of my weight. There wouldn't be combat fatigues big enough to fit me at 290 pounds. Wrong.! I was issued XXX fatigues and sent off to fight. A year in the heat and humidity. I didn't lose a pound. When it was time to come home, I ran into a problem. Soldiers leaving the war traded fatigues for khaki dress uniforms. They didn't come in XXX. The Army had fatigues big enough to send me to war, but didn't have a uniform my size so I could go home.. I was 20 years old but I had the body of a 55-year-old couch potato and had no business being at war but there I was with all the fit people.

Fat people are very angry. If we recruited fat people and unleashed them on the enemy, wars would be over in no time. As my old drill instructor used to say, "Men, It's not the Army, It's the people in the Army."

An action brought in federal court accuses radio station KAGE of violating provisions of the Civil Rights Act of 1964. The action filed by former KAGE reporter Tim Connelly and the Equal Employment Opportunity Commission alleges Connelly was fired for agreeing to take part in an investigation of a sex discrimination filed by another former KAGE employee. Connelly says his firing was in retaliation for that participation, which if proven, would violate Title VII of the Civil Rights Act. KAGE's attorney Paul Brewer said Connelly was not fired in retaliation for any testimony or assistance in the other suit.
The action Connelly agreed to participate in was filed by Paula Wiczek. She contends the station discriminated against her on the basis of sex because it granted a former male employee a two month leave of absence with pay for medical reasons. When she requested a maternity leave she was granted one month without pay. Her suit is pending.

Mr. Connelly, could you state your full name, spelling your last name for the court reporter?

Timothy Michael Connelly CONNELLY.

What's your address?

Winona, Minnesota.

Are you currently employed?

No.

Are you a student?

No

Have you attended Winona State University?

Yes

Did you obtain a degree?

Yes

What is that degree?

BA in Mass Communications

Have you ever been a party to a court action before?

No.

You have been sworn under oath and your testimony and my questions are taken down by a court reporter. The evidence and testimony given here and the questions and answers can be used in a legal procedure. It is important your answers be accurate. I understand you were a former employee of KAGE, Inc. is that correct?

Yes

When did you begin work there?

September, 1979

Prior to September, 1979 had you had any experience in radio broadcast work?

Yes

Where did you obtain that experience?

At KROC in Rochester, Minnesota.

What did you do at KROC?

It was a summer job I was a reporter and new writer. It was an internship.

How was the internship arranged?

I initiated it with the assistance of the Department of Vocational Rehab.

Are you disabled?

No, not now, no.

Have you ever been disabled?

What's this about? What's this have to do with me being fired?

I don't know.

Ms. Baron: I am going to object to the form of the question and ask consel to define what he means by "disabled" so that Mr. Connelly can respond.

Mr. Finch: Sure.

Mr. Connelly, what do you understand the word disabled to mean?

Handicapped in some way.

Do you understand it to mean a physical mental condition of some sort that interferes or is perceived with interfering with your ability to hold a job?

I could buy that.

Using that definition are you now or have you ever been handicapped?

MS. BARON: I am going to object. You are switching terms from disabled to handicapped.

MR. FINCH: Using that definition, are you now or have you ever been disabled?

Disabled in the sense that I was able to qualify for DVR help.

You qualified for help from the Department of Vocational Rehab because you were disabled?

I don't think of myself as disabled.

Did the Department of Vocational Rehab to your knowledge think that your were disabled?

You would have to talk with them.

What caused you to apply for help through the DVR

I was in a – a counselor referred me there.

Pardon?

A counselor referred me to the DVR

Who was that counselor?

A doctor. Dr. Duane Ollendick.

Now was he treating you for a disability?

No. Not that I know of.

Who does Mr. or Dr. Duane Ollendick work for?

Zumbro Valley Mental Health Center

Were you a patient at the Mental Health Center?

Out patient, I guess.

And you know the basis for you eligibility for services through the DVR?

Yeah, I guess.

What was the basis for you eligibility for services?

Emotional – emotional problems, I guess.

Were these service connected?

Not to my – no. Not to my knowledge.

What kind of emotional problems were these?

The doctor never gave me a diagnosis.

Were you ever hospitalized for these emotional problems?

No

Are you now receiving any kind of medications for these emotional problems?

No

During the time you were employed at KAGE have you ever been under a doctor's care for these emotional problems?

No

During the time you were employed by KAGE have you been taking any kind of medication?

No

Under a doctor's supervision?

No

How long did you work at KROC?

Two months.

What were your job duties?

I would usually rewrite stories. cover meetings such as city council, and help in the production work of the newscast.

What would you physically do to cover a meeting?

I would go to where the meeting was, and stay through the meeting and take notes and so forth and recordings and stuff like that, come back and write the story.

What kind of production work did you do?

Take the, say someone made a statement at a meeting, and I would take that and transfer it to a tape for the newscast, you know, for it to be played during the newscast, then I would help put together the news for the person that would be reading it.

Did you have any on the air responsibilities?

No.

Was this something you had trained for at College?

Right.

Can you tell me how you got your job at KAGE?

How I got my job at KAGE. KROC and KAGE traded stories off, and the news director at KROC knew I was coming down here to Winona State to go to school, so he contacted the news director down at KAGE, Steve Murphy, and said I might be of some help to him, and then I think I came down here during the summer, and visited the school and while I was here I stopped at KG and got an application, filled it out and sent a resume to Murphy, then I had an interview sometime in late July – maybe it was August '79 with Murphy, and he said he would have to check with management and so forth to see if it was okay. I told him I might be able to get some help through the DVR and so forth. I finally went to the DVR and they brought up the Tax Credit Program, a government program that would allow a tax break for the company, if they hired me. And I went down with a counselor. We talked to Mr. Ziebell and Mr. Murphy, and they interviewed me again, and then I was finally hired in September.

Okay. Prior to the time you went down to the station for the second time with the people from the DVR, or after you had contacted – first of all, did people from DVR happen to go with you to the station?

Not the first time.

Okay. The second time?

Yes

Prior to that time when you met with Mr. Ziebell, had you met with Mr. Ziebell during your first trip?

No.

So the first time you met with Mr. Ziebell was after the DVR had become involved.

To my knowledge.

What was your job title when you were hired at KAGE?

Newsman

Pardon?

Newsman

Did you receive a written statement of your duties or your job title?

No

How many hours per week were you assigned to work?

Twenty – we decided on twenty

About half time?

Right

During the first six months of your employment with KAGE, what were your responsibilities?

I covered school board meetings, county board meetings, and worked Sunday morning writing news. And I came in on the afternoons for a couple hours and helped out.

Did your job duties change over the time period that you were employed at KAGE?

I was given some air time, that I hadn't had before. But no, in essence there was no real change.

What does air time mean?

It's where you – you are on the air reading the news.

Previously you had not been on the air reading the news?

Not live, no

Had you been on air in a similar fashion other than live reading the news?

Once in awhile, not very regular, but I might give a 60 second report or something about some various thing.

This is the kind of thing that one sees or hears on broadcast news reports where this is Tim Connelly speaking to your from the fair?

Right.

Steve Murphy asked you to start doing some of these as part of your efforts to aquire some professional skills?

Right.

In Jan. 1981 you got air time, meaning you actually read the news over the air?

Right

What kind of newscast was that?

It was a ten minute local newscast on Sunday morning.

Who told you to do the newscast?

Mr. Ziebell

When did he tell you?

About two weeks before I started.

Did you have a meeting with him to discuss it?

Right

What happened in the meeting?

I had been covering a murder trial in Rochester the weeks previous, been sending reports back to KAGE, and he said that – you know, he was a little unsure at first of sending me, but then he thought my development was pretty good that he was going to give me the air time now, and he said, I think he said it was one the best decisions he had made, sending me to that – to that trial. He said that if, you know, If I kept developing, I could probably fit into the framework of the company, whatever.

He said you could fit into the framework of the company?

Yeah, if I kept, you know, the development up.

What did that mean??

Well, you know, I suppose it would mean more advancement if I kept developing the way I was.

Prior to that time, you talked to Mr. Ziebell about what was going to happen to you after you graduated from Winona State?

No, because at that time I didn't know if I was going to finish school.

Had you talked with him about what your were going to do after you completed your education?

No, not to my knowledge.

Okay. I understand that in the summer of 1980 there was an incident. Mr.
Murphy says there was an automobile accident in the Winona area that was reported to the station by someone and that you were reported to management to have made a remark, such as "we don't chase ambulances." Do you remember that incident?

Right

And I understand that a result of that, some of the people in management at KAGE were very unhappy with you, do you remember that?

Right

I think there was at this time even discussion of termination of your employment; is that correct?

Right

Did you attend a meeting with Mr. Murphy, Mr. Charles and Mr Ziebell present?

Right

In which that incident was discussed?

Right

What did Mr. Charles tell you at that meeting?

I don't remember.

Do you remember what Mr. Ziebell told you at that meeting?

No

You were told, were you not, that the management of the station was very unhappy about the attitude demonstrated by that remark?

That's what Mr. Ziebell said.

And I believe it was stated to you, was it not, that another incident like that and you would be terminated?

I don't recall.

And as I understand it, shortly after that meeting, within a month or so, Mr Murphy left and went to Minneapolis; is that correct?

Right

And after that, Mr. Ziebell assumed the responsibility for news direction, did he not?

Right

Who did you report to after Mr. Murphy left?

Doug Gehrke

Who is Doug Gehrke?

He is a full time news reporter at KAGE.

Did Mr. Ziebell from time to time after he began as news director talk to you about various assignments he had given you?

Yes

Did he talk to you about your performance?

Right

After this so-called ambulance chasing incident, do you understand what I mean by that?

Right

When you were alleged to have made this remark and this resulted in a conference in which you were told repetition of this would result in discipline? After that incident, did you put a cartoon up on the door of the newsroom?

No, I didn't put a cartoon up on the door, I don't believe.

Did you put up a drawing?

No, I didn't put a drawing up there.

Okay what did you put up on the door?

A collage

A collage. For the record, what is a collage?

It was a piece of cardboard with a lot of pictures on it.

Was there a message conveyed by this?

It was just some pictures on a piece of cardboard.

Were there any words written on this collage?

Only the words in the pictures.

Which were?

I don't really remember.

Did this have any reference to the ambulance incident?

It could have been related.

What do you mean "it could have been related?" Was it or wasn't it?

It happened soon afterwards.

Pardon?

It happened soon afterwards.

Was this intended to be a comment by you upon the station management or policies?

No, I don't believe so.

You said it could have had a relationship. Other than the temporal relationship in time, was there any message intended to be conveyed by the posting of this collage?

Just to relieve tension.

Pardon?

To relieve the tension.

Okay. And the collage was just some pictures, they had nothing to do with this incident; is that correct?

That's not what I said.

What was the relationship between the incident and the collage?

That it happened after the incident.

And aside from the temporal coincidence, the fact that this happened to be put on the door after the accident, the collage had nothing to do with this incident we've been discussing; is that correct?

It's after the fact.

Pardon?

It's – it was after the incident.

After the incident where you put a collage on the door, but it had nothing to do with the incident other than that?

No one told me to take it down.

I didn't ask that question. Is it a true statement that the collage had nothing to do with the incident in which it was reported that you had made this statement "we don't chase ambulances" and had been reprimanded for it?

I don't understand.

Okay. We will have to take this and break it down. Now as I understand it, you had a collage?

Right

And the collage consisted of pictures?

Right

And the pictures were pasted to what?

A piece of cardboard.

And there was no message on this except what was contained in the pictures?

I suppose the message would be the pictures.

The message would be the pictures. What did the pictures consist of?

Oh, there was some accident victims I believe, and some ambulances and so forth. That's all I can remember.

Okay. There was no lettering or words in those pictures?

There might have been. I don't remember. I didn't take a picture of it or anything.

Pardon?

I don't remember what the wording was.

And after the incident involving the ambulance incident where you were reprimanded, you placed this on the door to the news room; is that correct?

Yeah, sometime afterwards, I guess.

How long afterwards?

I don't remember.

Was it six months afterwards?

I don't think so.

Three months?

No

Two months?

No

One month?

I don't remember. It could have been a couple of weeks.

Do you think it was longer than one month?

No

When you posted that, did you intend that collage to be a statement about management policies at KAGE?

I don't know what I intended.

Pardon?

I don't know what I intended.

Did anybody involved in management of KAGE ever speak to you about the collage?

No

Do you think that the collage was meant to convey a message about the management policy that had been announced to you at the time you were reprimanded for the ambulance chasing incident we've been talking about.

Possibly.

Possibly?

I like cutting pictures out.

Pardon?

It was just a – it was a collage.

Sometime after the ambulance chasing incident we've been talking about, another reporter began working at KAGE, true?

Yes

Who was that reporter?

Melodie Ellefson

Were you asked to assist Ellefson to become familiar with the station?

I can't remember the small details. I suppose I was told to show her some of how it goes and how it works and so forth.

Did you assist her in becoming familiar with the activities of KAGE and the way in which the station operates?

I attempted.

You indicated there had been some conversations with Mr. Ziebell about your performance at KAGE. Did he ever tell you that he thought you had problems with your attitude toward the station?

There was only one thing I can remember that would indicate that possibly.

Do you remember giving an affadavit to the EEOC in this matter?

Right

You don't recall any conversation with Mr. Ziebell in which your attitude toward the station was discussed?

To my recollection, no

Was a schedule posted at KAGE detailing the assignments of various news staffers to attend meetings?

One week there was one

Did you write something on that notice?

Right

What did you write?

"What's this crap?"

Did you sign that?

I don't believe so.

Where was the notice at the time you wrote this on there?

It was on the desk of the newsroom.

And it was left there for everybody to see?

I don't know who it was left there for, it was just laying on the desk.

And you wrote the remark?

Right

And that remark stayed there in the newsroom after you left?

Right. Somebody pasted it on the bulletin board.

What did you mean by that statement, "What's this crap?"

What did I mean?

Yes

Just exactly what I said. "What's this crap?" There never had been a schedule before.

You weren't happy about the fact that there was a schedule?

I thought – I thought we were competent enough and professional enough and we had been doing it without a schedule, that we didn't need this type of –

My Question was, were you unhappy about the fact that a schedule had been made up?

I don't know. Unhappy, what do you mean by unhappy?

Did you like seeing a schedule? Were you pleased by it?

It was just there, and it was just my reaction.

You wrote your reaction on the sheet?

Right

And it somehow got put on the bulletin board?

Right

It wasn't on the bulletin board when you signed it?

No

Did Mr. Ziebell ask you about that statement at a meeting later on?

Right

He said to you, "Did you put this statement on this sheet?"

He knew I had done it, so you know, there wasn't any – tried to make believe I – like it was a big mystery who had done it, but he knew I had done it.

Was he happy about the fact that you had written that?

I don't know if he was happy.

Did he make a comment about it?

I believe he did.

What was the comment?

I really don't – I think he asked if I had done it or something like that.

Did he say something about it being unprofessional?

I don't recall.

Did he say something about it being inappropriate?

Possibly

You don't recall, but you think it might possibly have been the statement was inappropriate?

He was upset.

He was upset about it?

He was a little red in the face.

Red in the face?

I guess, yes.

Because he didn't like people writing things like "What's this crap?"on schedules that are posted in the newsroom?

I don't know what he likes.

Pardon?

I don't know what he likes.

All right. Did you gather from his demeanor and attitude at that time that he was unhappy about the fact that you had posted this remark in the news room?

I thought he was a little emotional.

You thought he was emotional.

Did you think at that time he might have been displeased with you?

I didn't think it was that big of thing.

Pardon?

I didn't think of the incident –

Can you listen to my question?

I didn't think much of it. I mean – I mean there was some disagreement there.

There was a disagreement?

I mean in philosophy.

In philosophy?

Right

Did you understand that Mr. Ziebell was displeased with your behavior?

I suppose you could gather that, yes.

Did you understand that he didn't want that kind of behavior to be repeated?

I believe so, yes.

There was a meeting on March 27th, what was its purpose?

Doug Gehrke was displeased with some of the writing. Melodie Ellefson had problems with her writing and problems in the news room with stories and stuff, it was just kind of a general bitch session or something like that.

Isn't true as a result of that meeting you reached some agreements as to what kind of writing styles were to be used and what kind of presentation formats were to be used?

I believe there was some agreement reached.

Were you ever told by David Ziebell after that meeting that you had not been following the agreements reached at that meeting?

No

I understand you know somebody named Paula Wiczek?

Right

I understand she has filed a charge with the Equal Employment Opportunity Commission, is that your understanding?

To my knowledge, yes.

And that has – is something to do with her pregnancy leave at KAGE, correct?

To my knowledge, that's what I know.

When did you first learn of that charge of discrimination?

Last summer.

At sometime Paula talked to you about the proceedings that had been going on before the EEOC involving that charge; is that correct?

Right

When did Paula talk to you?

March 30th

You make it a habit of recollecting dates accurately?

I am a reporter.

Did you have a face to face conversation?

No

Did she telephone you?

Yes

What did Paula Wiczek say to you during that conversation?

She said she had been to the Twin Cities for a hearing, and she wanted to know what type of program I had been on with the DVR. She wanted to know what type of program I had gotten and if I had gotten a raise last year.

What did you tell her?

I told her what the program was, and told her I didn't get a raise. And then we talked about some – she mentioned that during this hearing that KAGE had listed five or six employees that hadn't gotten raises because of unsatisfactory performance, and she named them off, and I was included, and she asked me if I would be willing to testify on her behalf if this came to trial or court or whatever it was, and I said yes.

What did she ask you to testify about?

About – about my pay status. About the program I was involved in I guess, and the fact that I, you know, why I didn't get a raise, why I did get a raise, something to that nature. I wasn't really clear on the facts. She just asked me if I would be willing if the time ever came.

I understand some time later you had a discussion with Darryl Smelser?

Right

You discussed the telephone call that you had received from Paula Wiczek; is that correct?

Right

Who is Smelser?

He is the sports director at KAGE.

How did the converation with Paula come up?

I was upset that they had put out this list of people especially Kathy Callahan and Darryl Smelser, because I knew how hard they worked, and I couldn't understand why they could be classified unsatisfactory. I asked Darryl, you know, if they had ever told him that, or if they had ever talked to him about it.

What was his response?

No

What did you say then?

I think I told him that I probably would testify for Paula if the time came up or something, or in Paula had talked to him at all, that's all I can really remember.

Pardon?

That's all I can really remember.

In your affidavit you say that thereafter, Mr. Smelser was called in to Mr. Ziebell's office, is that correct?

I can't remember.

Pardon?

Darryl told me he was called into someone's office.

Did he tell you what went on in there?

He just said that they had told him there was – not to believe the rumors that were being spread about this unsatisfactory work performance, and he had been doing a good job.

Did he tell you, at any time, if he had ever said anything to Mr. Ziebell or any other representative of the station management, about your conversation with him concerning Paula Wiczek's telephone call?

Not to my knowledge.

You had a conversation with Mr. Ziebell a few days later and he made a statement about Paula Wiczek's phone call?

Yes

How long did that conversation last/

A long time.

A long time?

You knew at that time what Mr. Smelser had reported to you about what had been told to him during his meeting with Ziebell?

I believe so, yes.

You also talked about your school work during that meeting?

I believe we did.

You talked about the interference between your school work and your job?

I don't know if we – I don't think we mentioned interference. I don't understand what you are talking about.

Did you talk about problems in coordinating your work schedule and your school schedule during that meeting?

No

You didn't?

Not that I recall.

Did you talk about your school work during that conversation?

If we did, it was just a very short thing that I wanted – that I wanted to finish school.

Did you talk about the performance of the news department at KAGE?

That might have come up, yes.

Did you tell him you were dissatisfied with the news department at KAGE?

I might have said there was room for improvement.

Did you talk about your dissatisfaction with Melodie Ellefson?

I may have mentioned that yes.

What did you tell him?

I said that she wasn't working up to my expectations or she should be – she should be farther than she is in progressing. She seemed to be lacking.

Lacking in what?

Doing the basic news jobs, in my mind.

Lacking – did you tell him what your problem was with her?

I guess he said that this is a small marker town and it's a place for beginners, and we have to expect mistakes and so forth. But I said if I had made that many mistakes by now, I would probably be fired.

You said that?

I believe I did.

Did Mr. Ziebell talk to you during this conversation about his opinion of your attitude towards the station's management?

I guess he asked me what my attitude towards management was, or if I trusted management.

He didn't criticize your attitude in any way, did he?

I guess if him saying I wasn't committed to KAGE was criticism, I imagine that would be.

Could you tell me what the Mississippi Queen is?

To my knowledge it is a bar down the street from here.

Do they advertise on KAGE?

I don't know. I'm not in sales.

Do you ever listen to KAGE?

Rarely.

Did you overhear broadcasts while you were in the studios?

I was working.

My question was, did you listen to it?

Well it's playing, you know you can't help.

Yes, you listened to it?

It was in the air, I suppose it went through my ears.

You heard it?

I imagine, yes.

Did you ever see the commercial logs around the station?

Laying on the desks, but I never read them.

So you have no idea whether the Mississippi Queen might have been a sponsor on KAGE?

No, my job was in the news department.

And you had no idea that they might have been a sponsor?

No, I didn't. I didn't know who the sponsors were.

Did you write a news story for delivery over KAGE concerning a hit and run driver who turned herself in to the Winona police?

Right

Did that news item, as you wrote it, make reference to the Mississippi Queen?

Right

Do you remember what that reference was?

That the woman and her friend had been drinking at the Winona bar called the Mississippi Queen or something to that effect.

Did you ever have any conversations with Melodie Ellefson about using the name of the establishment in that story?

Not to my recollection.

Did you ever have any conversations with Pete Lehken about using the name of the Mississippi Queen in that story?

The next day I talked to him.

What did Lehken say to you?

I guess he said – he called me a fool for using it or something.

Pardon?

He called me a fool or dummy for using it in the story.

What did you say to him?

I thought it was a journalistic thing to do in my opinion.

How did the subject come up?

He was standing in the hall and I asked his opinion.

Were you in the habit of going up to Lehken and asking his opinion about using things in news stories?

No

But on this occasion you did?

Yes

Were you unhappy about the fact that the name Mississippi Queen had been crossed out of the news copy of the story?

I don't know if I was unhappy.

You didn't care that the name Mississippi Queen had been crossed out of that news story?

I didn't think it was right.

Were you angry about it?

No anger, no

You disagreed with the decision to cross out the name?

Right

What were your scheduled work hours during that day?

I didn't punch a clock. I didn't know. I just – I didn't have a schedule that I followed.

You didn't have a schedule?

I had a routine.

What was your routine?

I came in about 1:30, 2:00 o'clock, then there was city council that night, and that starts at 7:00. I came in, I think I left early because of city council.

Did you have a conversation with David Ziebell on that day?

Maybe about 2:00 o'clock he came in.

Isn't true he asked you what you were doing?

I think so.

He asked you why you weren't working or something?

I was waiting to be briefed.

Did he brief you?

Not really.

Did he talk to you about some news assignments to work on?

We chatted about a few ideas.

And didn't you understand that that was a briefing?

It hadn't been like the briefings I had been getting for the last year and a half.

Who had been giving you those briefings for the last year and a half.

Either Steve Murphy or Doug Gehrke.

And they weren't there at the time?

Doug was on vacation.

Who else was there?

Melodie Ellefson.

Did you turn in any stories that day?

Yes

When did you turn the story in?

No, it wouldn't be that day. It would be the next day technically. It was the early morning of the next day. About 1a.m.

When was the next conversation you had with Dave Ziebell/

The next day.

How did you happen to talk to him?

I have classes on Tuesday and Thursday afternoons, and I usually call in to see if they want any meetings covered that night, and he told me to come in, he wanted to talk to me.

And you went into the station?

Right

You went into Mr. Ziebell's office?

I waited for him to show up.

What happened then?

He called me into his office.

Was anybody else present?

No

What did he say to you?

As far as I can remember, he said that it was obvious that I wasn't happy there anymore, and it was best that I leave, for all interested parties, and he said I hadn't written any stories the day before, and I think – I can't remember that much of it, and he told me to hand in my key and my time schedule, and that was it.

He told you, did he not, about the remarks you had made or alleged to have made during the conversation with Lehken?

No

What was your response when he told you to turn in your time card and your keys?

I put my key on the desk, and told him he could keep his money.

What did you do then?

I think I went to the newsroom and picked up my books, and then told everybody in the place I was fired, and went.

Did you tell then why you were fired?

I didn't know why I was fired.

How did you tell them?

I yelled.

How did you yell?

As I was going out the door I shouted "I'm fired everybody."

Anything else?

Not that I can recall.

Did you have any conversations with Doug Gehrke about your termination?

Yes

What did you tell him?

He wanted to know why I was fired.

And what did you tell him?

I told him that I was – that I guess that they told me I was unhappy there.

What caused you to seek counseling at the Zumbro Valley Mental Health Center?

I don't think it is relevant to this firing.

What?

I don't think it is relevant to the issue here.

You might be right, but we don't know until you answer the question?

I was dissatisfied with the way my life was going.

Had you been required to seek counseling as a result of any kind of court action or agreement made in regard to any court action?

No.

We talked about this collage that was on the door to the newsroom. That was in fact on the back of the door, wasn't it?

Right

So that management wouldn't see it?

I thought the back of the door was a good place for it.

And in fact management couldn't see ot. unless they were in the news roon when the door was shut, could they?

That's when they would see it, probably.

And this collage had a lot of words on it like "gore" and "blood?"

I don't recall.

Pictures of bloody accidents?

Yes

Some kind of references to ambulances?

Yeah

Did you ever tell Melodie Ellefson that you were dissatisfied with management at KAGE?

Possibly, I might have.

Isn't it true that you told people quite often that you were dissatisfied with some aspect of management at KAGE, particularly your fellow employees?

Well, as far as I know, it's freedom of speech, free country.

Is that a true statement that you told them quite frequently of your dissatisfaction with the management and operation of KAGE?

What's frequent?

Did you tell them once a week or oftener?

Possibly

Certainly more than once a month?

I can't remember.

Did you ever tell Melodie Ellefson not to go out on calls involving accidents?

I don't think I did.

You received in the mail sometime after you were terminated a statement regarding the reasons for your termination, did you not?

Right

What did you receive?

I received a carbon copy form from the employment office saying that I wasn't qualified for unemployment because of misconduct, then it gave uncooperative behavior, demeanor, so forth and so forth.

Did you follow the guidelines for writing news stories?

I wrote news stories.

What?

I wrote my news story the way I write my news story.

Did you go along with the guidelines that had been agreed upon?

When I felt they were appropriate.

And when you didn't feel they were appropriate, you didn't go along with them?

In my mind it was just an experiment.

My question is, and when you felt that they were not appropriate, you did not go along with them?

Right

Do you have a driver's license now?

No

Did you ever have a driver's license?

Military

Did you ever have a civilian driver's license anywhere?

No'

The Direct Examination by Ms Barton EEOC

Mr. Connelly, I have some questions.

When you were hired at KAGE on this special program, what was your rate of pay?

I believe it was minimum wage, 2.90 at the time,

And did you ever get any raises?

Just when minimum wage went up.

What was your pay rate at the time you were terminated?

$3.35 an hour.

Did you work more than 20 hours a week?

Yes after Steve Murphy left, they didn't replace him right away, so I had to fill in more hours and I averaged out about 30 hours a week.

And were you paid at the same minimum wage rate for the additional time?

Right

Did you ever work more hours than you turned in on your time sheet?

Yes

Did anyone know you were working those additional hours?

Yes

Who?

Steve Murphy I would say. I believe Doug Gehrke. My co-workers knew I was putting in the hours.

Did Ziebell know your were putting in the additional hours?

I think he did.

Did he ever mention it to you?

Yes he did.

How would that have come about?

In the ambulance incident, in that meeting, during that meeting after the ambulance incident.

What was said?

I said, " You know how many hours I've been putting in, working hard," and he says, "Yes, we know, but that's irrelevant," something like that.

At the time of that ambulance incident, was there anyone else in the news room when it was reported?

Right

Who?

Doug Gehrke.

Who reported it by the way?

A sales person.

And did Mr. Gehrke say anything at the time it was reported?

I think we discussed whether we would go to the scene of the accident or not.

And did you go to the scene?

Right

When?

It must have been a half hour later, maybe, we went to the scene of the accident.

And did you ever write up the accident as a news story?

Right

Who did that?

Doug, I think he did it. He got the information from the police that were there at the scene, I believe he wrote the story up.

Did the story go on the air.

Yes

Did Ziebell have conversations with you on occasion?

Yes, kind of pep talks, keep up the good work and so forth, work on a few things.

Did Ziebell ever ask you to tell him if things were going badly or if things were bothering you at the news room?

I think he did. I think he might have said that I should come to him with problems if I felt like it.

Let's talk about that collage for moment. You said that you pasted the collage up on the door. Did Ziebell see that collage?

Yes

And what was his reaction when he saw it the first time?

He laughed.

Did Mr. Charles see that collage?

Yes, he did.

And what was his reaction if you were there to observe it?

I believe he chuckled too or something, sneered. It wasn't – it was kind of a light hearted type of thing.

Were there also pictures of other people other than bloody accident victims?

Right

What were those?

I think there were some pin up girls, like bikinis and stuff like that.

Did either Mr. Ziebell or Mr. Charles or anyone else in management ask you to take that collage down?

No

Was it clear from the outset that you had done the collage and posted it?

I brought it into the building. I don't know, it wasn't really clear, it wasn't signed by anybody.

You didn't sign your name to it?

No

How long did that collage stay up on the door?

A very long time. Maybe three or four months.

Who took it down, if you know?

I think Doug might have been cleaning up the office, he might have taken it down. We decided it was time for it to go.

But no one in management ordered it to be taken down?

No

You had a meeting with Ziebell after you had spoken with Paula Wizcek.

Yes

What was Ziebell's demeanor?

He appeared upset. He seem concerned about something.

And did he come right out and ask you about Paula Wiczek?

Yes

And what did you say?

I said I had been in contact with her and had heard about the unsatisfactory work thing and I asked him about that. He told me there wasn't any truth to that.

Did he day anything more about Paula Wiczek?

He said she was just trying to harass the people at the station, and that she lied a lot, and he kind of – he ran her down.

Did he give you any advice?

He said I wouldn't benefit with any association with Paula Wiczek.

What did you say?

I believe that – I really didn't – I said something like I'm not a fool or
something. I really can't – like I'm no fool or something like that. Or I
know what you are talking about or something like that.

What did you think he was talking about?

I think he was threatening me. That's what I thought at the time you
know. Get involved with her, and that's it.

Mr. Connelly, did you serve in the armed forces?

Yes

What dates?

1968 to 1972

Did you serve overseas?

MR FINCH: I object to that as irrelevant.

Yes

Were you in Vietnam?

Yes

MR. FINCH: I object as irrelevant and ask it be stricken.

When did you seek an outpatient counselor at the Mental Health Center?

1977, I believe.

Were you in school at that time?

I was at Mankato State.

And what were you majoring in?

Health – and I believe it was health and emergency room care or something like that.

Were you referred to DVR for anything specific?

Job counseling, testing. skills testing and so forth.

Why?

Because the counselor I was talking to at the Mental Health Center felt that these people could get me going or help me out more than he could, in some way.

And DVR did send you for testing, is that correct?

They tested me.

And what were the results of those tests?

There were a number of tests. The vocational test showed that I had a high interest in reporting and literature and so forth. I talked with the counselor and we decided that I would go to community college and start taking some classes in journalism and so forth.

And you did ultimately get a degree in mass communications?

Right

MR FINCH RECROSS EXAMINATION

How old are you Mr. Connelly

32

Are you married?

No

You said that Mr Ziebell told you to come to him with problems, if you had any?

I believe he did.

You didn't go to him with problems, did you?

I didn't feel he was my father confessor.

Mr Gehrke was present in that news room on the date of the ambulance chasing incident?

Yup.

Mr. Gehrke didn't tell anybody that you didn't chase ambulances, did he?

I don't believe he said it.

How often did you meet with Mr. Ziebell during your employment at KAGE?

Maybe a dozen times.

On those occasions, were you scared when you were in his office?

I don't think so, no.

Did you ever tell employees when you went into his office you thought you were going to be fired?

Well, I may have after the ambulance incident.

Did you ever tell Melodie Ellefson that you thought you might be fired when you went into his office?

Jokingly I might have said it.

Were you laughing at the time?

Some people do have a sense of humor.

Did anybody ever tell you that your sense of humor might be sarcastic?

Yeah.

Did Ziebell ever tell you that your sense of humor was sarcastic?

Not that I recall.

Did he ever tell you he didn't like your sarcastic remarks?

I think he said I should keep my mouth shut in certain situations.

When Ziebell called you to his office in early April, you could tell, couldn't you, that he was visibly upset?

He had the look.

He had the look?

That he was concerned about something.

You thought he was concerned about something. Was he angry?

No, not really angry, no.

Was his face red?

I don't recall.

Was his voice loud?

No, I don't believe so.

Did he sound irritated?

Possibly, yes.

And nobody else was present?

No

And you didn't tell anybody after that meeting that he had made these remarks to you?

Yes, I told others.

Who did you tell?

Friends at school.

Did you tell anybody at the station?

I may have talked to my co-workers.

How many more hours did you put in than you reported on your time sheets?

Maybe, 10, 15 hours more a week.

What were you during that time that you weren't reporting?

I was working.

Working where?

I only got 20 hours a week, so I would work 30 and I thought I was only getting paid for 20. I might have put in eight hours a day but I only put down four hours a day, because I was only allowed 20 hours a week I thought.

Who only allowed you 20 hours?

That's what agreed on when I started work.

You were hired for 20 hours a week?

To my knowledge, right.

Was there a time you were getting paid for more than 20 hours a week?

During the summer or after Steve Murphy left the station.

Did somebody tell you you could be paid for more than 20 hours after he left?

I believe Ziebell said I could put down more hours.

Did Ziebell ever tell you not to put down the time. That you wouldn't be paid for time that you were working?

No

You stated that Ziebell knew that your were putting in more hours than were being reported on your time sheet?

Right

How did Ziebell know that?

He was operations manager.

My question, sir, is how did he know that?

I don't know how he knew it, but he mentioned it, and he acknowleged that he knew it.

When did he acknowledge that he knew that?

In the meeting we were having after the ambulance incident thing.

And exactly what did he say?

I said, you know how many hours I have been putting in and working hard and overtime and stuff, and he acknowledged, yes we do. But he didn't take that into account when firing me and stuff, you know.

This was during the conversation in which you were defending yourself against this charge that you had made the ambulance chasing remark and it was unprofessional and showed a poor attitude, and I said you know how hard I have been working, how many hours I have been putting in, and he said I know, but that's beside the point, is that it?

Yeah

Was there anything in that remark to indicate that he knew you were working more than twenty hours a week?

Well I was at the station all the time, so they must have realized that I was.

You were at the station all the time?

Not all the time, but quite a bit of the time.

Did you sleep there?

I probably might have well – no, I didn't sleep there.

Did anyone else know you were working more time than reported?

I have no idea.

No more questions.

Redirect Examination by MS. Baron

Did Mr. Ziebell say that Melodie Ellefson was hurting your work performance?

He said she was making some mistakes. I don't recall anything about her affecting my work performance.

Did he say anything to you about your work performance?

Just the part about commitment. Then he said I was a good reporter and everything and so forth, but that I didn't seem I was committed to KAGE, and he wanted to know what I was committed to.

You state here that you told him you gave up study time to work late nights?

Right

And by dropping out of school during the winter quarter because of work. What did he say to that?

I don't recall.

No further questions.

A Winona radio station has been cleared of charges it illegally fired a reporter. The judge dismissed the suit filed by Tim Connelly and said Connelly failed to present persuasive proof he was fired for agreeing to take part in a sex discrimination suit filed by a co-worker. The judge concluded that the case rested on nothing more than the former reporter's assertions.

Connelly asserted that station news director Dave Ziebell said "he(Connelly) would not profit from his association with the woman who filed the law suit. Connelly was fired 12 days after talking with Ziebell.

Tim has returned to the MHC once again with his vague complaints. The precipitating event this time is that there has been a change in news editors at the radio station. The new editor is an "idiot" according to Tim. What this tends to do to Tim is make him feel less worthwhile, less able to function properly, and less likely to be assertive and utilize what he already knows and has. It is very nearly impossible to get from Tim what specifically he is looking for by coming to the MHC. He states that he knows that this is a crisis for him, but has no specific therapeutic goal. At this point in time, given the fact that he is asking for ongoing sessions, but is unable to verbalize a goal, I have agreed to meet with him for a supportive relationship. He indicates very clearly that he has no one outside to talk with and needs a place for supportive communication. JW:

9-3
Tim is very vague once again today. He says that he is absolutely blank when he arrives here and has nothing to think about or talk about. I inquire as to whether or not he could profit from some means of written focusing and went over a journaling method with him. He seemed interested and took notes that I shared with him. I explored with him the use of medication as a possibility today and he refuses this. He says he does not "need it right now." I attempted to learn more about him and his history today. He says he is reticent to share anything. One can only infer from his comments that what memories he has of his growing up years are unpleasant. JW:

9-11

Tim has begun to share some information regarding his past and his family today. In high school he ran around with ten other high school boys. He had no particular goals and describes himself as a fairly typical adolescent who was not interested in going to college and would go off to the country with the boys occasionally and drink beer and smoke some cigars. After high school he moved out of the family home five months later and took an apartment in Rochester with a friend until he went into the Army about a year later. He went on to describe his mother and father. Mother was described as a fairly typical housewife/mother until he went into the Army.
At that time she stopped her mothering role to some degree and went into the work force. His father worked in a local grocery store. He sees his father as a relatively low inertia individual who he is probably the most like.
What emerges today is a picture of a man who moved very slowly through career opportunities inspite of his talents and abilities. It is almost as though he were moving slowly so as to consolidate his ground because of his own personal lack of sense of security. He tends to use his creativity more in service to other people by producing for them than he does in investing for himself. The hypothesis here is that if he did move with his creativity he would possibly move more quickly than he is able to feel comfortable with. JW:

9-18

Once again Tim has little or nothing to say. His expectations of therapy are very mixed. He is both impatient for results and yet at the same time expects practically nothing to happen initially. JW:

9-25

Mr. Connelly and I talked at some length about his own self-perspective. He says the dismissal from the Winona radio station as the beginning of beginning to feeling about himself as though he were a failure. What was most damaging were the depositions taken because he went ahead and sued his former employer. In the depositions, people accused him of not doing anything, of only reading newspapers while he was supposed to be working and one woman described him as colorful as a door knob. He found these accusations very hurting and harmful and has questioned himself about his effectiveness as a person ever since. He has very little ability to see his own resources and I have invited him to consider some hypnotic work which may assist him in going around some of the ego defenses that he has. He sees himself as being a very fragile person and is very apprehensive whenever talking about his own self perspective. JW:

!0-9

Tim today feels somewhat freer to talk and describes himself to me as someone who sees literally no opportunities. He is able to relate this to his developmental years where his parents created an ultimate goal of growing up, moving to the city and finding a job with one of the major employers and that would be his ultimate achievement. He translates this into a personal philosophy of "life is tough, and then you die." He became more animated as the hour went on was about to share more and verbalize more.

10-17

Mr. Connelly today presents an entirely different picture. he came in and told me that his whole week has been very negative. He sites two examples of it being a negative week. He sites the Viking's losing and having the sheriff tell him that any wages he makes will be garnisheed. He kept this up for a period of some 10 or 15 minutes before he told me that he paid off the unpaid college debt. This caused me to question much of how he handles relationships and particularly the therapeutic relationship. My interpretation of this is that he tends to keep people at an emotional distance with his wit and flare for dramatic presentation. I am once again at the point of considering hypnotherapy with him; however, he remains very skeptical about it and this may just exclude any utilization of this as a technique. JW:

10-24

Tim has indicated today that seeing him on a Wednesday is much better than a Monday or Tuesday. He states that Mondays and Tuesdays he is scarcely functional. This caused me to raise some questions about his chemical use. He reminded me that his original contact with the mental health center was because he was concerned about his chemical use. Based on earlier notes, it was obvious that it was not thought that he was chemically dependent. There has been an increase in his McAndrews of two points. The last interpretation was that he was possibly misusing alcohol For this reason, I am referring him to Dr. Carl West for a further evaluation of chemical use. Tim has begun to become more conversant during the sessions now. It appears that he is less passive and less likely to sit back and await a "feeding" of psychotherapy. It is obvious that he is becoming more and more an integral part of the process. Today he talks about a fear and apprehension that seems to step in whenever we have discussed a strategy that he might be able to use. Tim seems to respond to the notion that the fear and apprehension is protecting him in some fashion but is uncertain as to what that apprehension requires in order to allow him to move further ahead in terms of personal investigation of things he may do to improve his own situation. JW:

11-25

Tim and I reviewed what he has been doing since his last appointment. I have continued with my dire predictions of him being unable to resolve his situational depression in less than a month, and have told him to take his time. He appears to become somewhat more animated when presented with this information from me, and though he claims to be depressed, appears to have a fairly good mood considering his recent loss of his job. He has talked about different options for the future and I reframed his firing as a possibility of starting over in something he really wants to do. We spent some time talking about his upcoming dinner at Thanksgiving at his sisters', at which time he expects to be abused and humiliated by the family because he is not currently working. We talked about his choice to go there and put up with that as an example of his continuing to offer himself as a doormat for other people. I informed him that it may be necessary for him to continue being a doormat for a while. Tim continues to look less depressed while report feeling down. He has been active, continuing to walk and catch the bus wherever he goes. He has not actively looked for work, though he has been to the unemployment office. I will continue with a pessimistic approach with this man, as I think encouraging him to do better may serve a paradoxical end.

12-3

Tim continues to express feelings of hopeless and helplessness. He related that his experience at Thanksgiving with his family was much less aversive than he had expected, as they did not grill him about not having a job. He states that he was initially uncomfortable in that circumstance, but gradually felt better about being there. We talked in some detail about his lack of connection with other people, and the fact that this is an important dynamic in his inability to get accurate feedback about himself. We also discussed the possibility of him doing some vocational testing to try to determine his current interests and aptitudes. Overall this is a fairly bland session. Tim is showing no actual signs of depression, though he states that he feels bad. He has shown little initiative at this point in looking for other employment, as he appears to believe that no matter what he does he will be a failure. We will continue working on the present treatment plan goals of trying to find ways that Tim can avoid being treated like a doormat. CW:

12-12

At the beginning of this session Tim and I reviewed his efforts to keep busy, given that he is unemployed. It is clear that he is doing very little active looking for a job, as he appears to have little hope that he will soon be employed again. He spends his days getting up late, obtaining newspapers and chatting with a few people downtown, and then returning home to read his papers and watch MTV. He stated that he feels that he must break out of this routine soon, but I told him that he may not be ready to do so. The subject of his interpersonal style was discussed in some detail, particularly his tendency to isolate himself. I related this to feelings of shame that he might have, and this led to a discussion of his being overweight. When he was talking about being overweight and feeling shame about that he had tears in his eyes, the first sign of sadness that I've seen in him despite him many losses. He also lost his shoulder shrugging blank look during this time.

It appears that Tim's sense of futility is related to some deep sense of shame, perhaps related to his weight and early rejection he experienced in his family. The plan is to try to further explore with Tim the same issue, particularly as it relates to his lack of self-worth and passivity. CW:

12-18

Today's session started with a review of how Tim is spending his time. He voices frustration and anger at himself for not doing more. Much of the time was spent today in discussing feelings and appropriate labels for those feelings. It was clear that Tim has considerable difficulty in doing this, and this inability may contribute to some confusion on his part. We focused on shame and explored possible origins of shame in his life, particularly talking about his family and history of failed vocational attempts. He spoke more today than in any session since I've begun seeing him, but continues to maintain a fairly passive approach to therapy, and described the therapy process as being on in which the two of us, working together, might discover barriers to his living his life the way he wants to, and further described therapy as similar to setting together a jigsaw puzzle, the picture of which is not known beforehand. This description appears to appeal to his intellectual curiosity and seemed non-threatening to him. For the first time today Tim appears to have some appreciation for the fact that he does continue to have choices in his life. He was interested in the story I told him about a 62 year old former client who, after 40 years of impairment, turned his life around and is now living a very contented life. The plan is to continue the same slow paced approach with a focus on feeling rather than a specific behavior change. CW:

12-31

The beginning of this session was spent in reviewing with Tim what he had been doing over the holiday. He has made some changes, i.e. sending out two resumes and being involved with some friends who came over to wish him holiday greetings. However, he minimizes these changes and sees himself to be in the same rut he's been in. We talked about the difficulty that exists for someone to accept the affection and respect of others, when they do not like or respect themselves. This led into a discussion of an early childhood experience related to an apparent failure for Tim to establish basic self esteem and self respect. Numerous early incidents were recalled, with particular emphasis on Tim's father's alcoholism. It was learned that Tim preferred to spend time with his mother and grandmother, and he acknowledges having wished that his father was like the fathers of his friends. He seemed somewhat guilty about acknowledging this, but he was given substantial support for sharing these feelings. He continues to be fairly quiet during session, but seems to be quite interested in what transpires during therapy. Tim showed somewhat less depression than in the past. He seems interested in the process of therapy, but continues to manifest little optimism about possible change in the future. It appears that he continues to expect to be rejected by others, and to eventually fail, so there is little reason to look for a catalyst in his life to effect substantial change. The plan is to continue the present treatment plan with emphasis on self esteem issues and a search for a catalyst for change

1-14

Today's session open with a discussion of what might be necessary to serve as a catalyst for change in Tim's behavior and feeling. We talked about his long standing sense of hopelessness, and we discussed the connection between affect and perception. Tim has had some positive experience in tha he has made the first cut on a job which he has applied for in the Twin Cities. About 70 people applied for this job and at the present time he is among the 18 surviving candidates. He reported that he didn't believe he did well in the telephone interview, though he said that his assessment of his ability is not very clear. We talked about specific tasks (listing former jobs, and their pluses and minuses, and looking in the dictionary of occupational titles for descriptions of possible new jobs) which he might pursue since he has time to do that. He didn't appear enthusiastic about this, and it appears to be unlike him to attempt new things. He continues to exhibit considerable pessimism and ambivalence and does not appear to want to try anything which might fail. This seemed to keep him stuck. Tim continues to not appear depressed, though he notes some problem with sleep. He has trouble going to sleep, but after doing so usually sleeps about six hours. He says that the amount of exercise he is getting has gone down, primarily because of the winter weather. I encouraged him to resume as much exercise as he could. It does not appear necessary to consider medication at the present time because of his minor sleep problems. He continues to be pessimistic and ambivalent about the future and has maintained his expectations of failure. The plan is to continue chipping away at Tim's self statements, his feelings of failure, and his perception and expectation of a life of continuing sadness and lack of fulfillment. CW:

1 – 21

As usual Mr. Connelly was fairly quiet during this session. I focused my remarks primarily on his isolation, his unwillingness to take even small risks, and his assumptions about what other people think of him. He says that he is a person very reluctant to take risks, and he also admits that his apathy may be misinterpreted by others as patience. He acknowledges becoming more and more lethargic, spending many hours each day in front of the television. He states that this is not comfortable for him, but that he perceives it to be a more positive alternative than to actually explore different alternatives for his life. When asked what he was getting out of the therapy sessions, he stated that he was getting feedback, but could not be more specific that that. It is not exactly clear what, if anything, Tim is accomplishing by coming to therapy. It does appear to be his only real contact with other people, as most of his other relationships are quite superficial. There has been very little actual behavior change noted, and this therapist is experiencing some frustration with Tim's passivity. The plan is to staff this case with Tim's former therapist, JW, and any other available members of the adult staff. There is some reason to question whether or not continued therapy with no apparent results is useful to him. he does not appear willing at this time to accept responsibility for changing his way of doing things. CW:

3-4

Today Mr. Connelly continued to explore in a fairly open manner his difficulty in following through on plans which may be of some use to him. He was able to identify the feelings of embarrassment, emptiness, and fear as being an interference or a block to his following through on specific goals. We reviewed the avoidance paradigm explanation which he appears to understand fairly well. He was given the metaphor of jumping from a burning plane as an example of how it might be important to do things which may be useful despite fear. Once again we identified the responsibility for his change being this, particularly his willingness to run some risks of rejection and failure. Tim continues to be verbal and involved in the therapy process. He has not followed through on any of the possible things he might do, but is clearer about the usefulness of having more contact with people, becoming involved in possible volunteer work and in more actively seeking jobs. The plan is to continue with the present strategy of helping him identify feelings which interfere with him accomplishing his goals. CW:

3-12

Today's session focused on attempting to identify with Tim the antecedents of his feelings which prevent him from following through on specific goals or behaviors which might be useful to him. We concentrated on a rational-immotive strategy of attempting to identify negative self statements which he may use which increase his anxiety, embarrassment, and pessimism. He had some difficulty doing this, though appeared to be able to recognize that he says things to himself which increase his perception of being rejected by other people. He did a good job of formulating a list of life circumstances which he must meet in order to feel some contentment. Tim was once again an active participant in the therapy process. He appears to be understanding the concepts of avoidance, feelings which prevent action, and self statements which may lead to those feelings. He also has voluntarily done some homework which appears to indicate a more active interest in the therapy program. The plan is to follow up with the identification of negative self statements, and begin to replace them with positive statements about himself in order to reduce his interfering negative feelings. I will also be writing a letter to DVR at his request to summarize current treatment. CW:

3-19

This session was spent in discussing in some detail with Tim the diagnosis of avoidant personality disorder. This topic came ip when I asked him if he had read the copy of the letter sent to him regarding the evaluation requested by Voc Rehab. He stated that it was the first time he had read anything about him by a therapist and he seemed to have numerous questions regarding the diagnosis, treatment, and prognosis for outcome. This appeared to be useful avenue for Tim beginning to understand that he is not psychotic, but that he suffers from a major personality disorder of a fairly long term duration. He seemed to recognize that his other symptoms (depression and anxiety) may be related to his avoidant personality style. He was quite verbal during the session, though he continues to do some blocking. I interpreted this to him as his expectation that his questions would be perceived by me as inappropriate of silly. He acknowledges this is true, but has difficult time not censoring himself. Tim seems to show good understanding of the personality disorder diagnosis. He also seems to understand the treatment strategy of a cognitive behavioral approach aimed at helping him interrupt negative self statements and to examine some of his assumptions about himself and life in general. It appears that therapy is moving along much better than it had before the frank discussion with him a few weeks ago concerning his own lack of participation. The plan is to continue the present strategy of being very direct with Tim about the nature of his disorder and specific with him regarding the treatment plan.

3-26

The beginning of this session was a review of the avoidant personality diagnosis. We spent some time talking about the feelings that interfere with Tim's ability to tolerate interactions with other people. He voices some frustration that he is not doing anything, but acknowledges that he feels empty, overwhelmed, and anxious when he thinks about being more active and looking for hobs and considering volunteer work. He voices pessimism and hopelessness again this session, but appears to be more willing to look at the underlying feelings which may involve guilt and shame. Tim continues to be pretty much in the same spot that he has been in over the past few weeks. He is more active in therapy, appears to trust me more, and is more willing to examine the relationship between the two of us. He says, "I don't know" much less often than he has in the past, though he continues to exhibit some blocking in thought process. The plan is to continue the present treatment plan, though it appears that a treatment plan review may be useful since the diagnosis has changed to avoidant personality disorder. This will be done over the next two weeks. CW:

6-19

Tim was about 15 minutes late to the appointment. He apparently had some difficulty with his time schedule and the bus and ended up walking on a very hot day. He has done several very surprising things over the past week, including the following: backing away from some interpersonal conflict on his current temp job, interviewing with two other employment agencies about other possible temp jobs, going to the local newspaper to pick up two books to review, going to the college radio station to talk with the manager about what it took to do his job. Tim reports that he feels very good about having done these things, though he is somewhat surprised that he was able to complete these tasks. He attributes it to just having a good day. However, I told him I thought it was directly related to improving self concept, and changing assumptions about his limitations. Tim clearly is doing much better than he has been in the past. His sense of humor has increased substantially, his energy level is also improved, and most importantly he is interacting at a much more effective level with other persons. We talked at some length about continuing to explore the origins of some of his assumptions about himself and to look at what has interfered with his growth with respect to interpersonal relationships. The plan is to continue the current treatment strategy, that of supporting Tim's growth and gently investigating the origins of his hypersensitivity to criticism from other people. CW:

6-26

Tim reports some periods of depression over the past week. He states that he is not as energized as he has been. I advised him that I thought this was to be expected, as it may be a reaction to his higher frequency risk taking behavior in the prior week. Considerable time was spent in looking at the messages that Tim has had regarding success. He had a very difficult time identifying the things about himself that he didn't like, became involved in a lot of thought blocking and inability to complete sentences. While he finds it more convenient to state that he hates other things, such as the weather and the city in general, he does acknowledge that one of the most frustrating things for him is his own inability to alter his current situation. We talked about different definitions of success, and the difficulty that occurs when an individual believes that he or she should not make any mistakes. Tim was very involved in today's discussion and appears to be diligently trying to understand what keeps him from clearly identifying his own needs and feelings, and keeps him from working towards getting those needs met. It did not appear that Tim was as depressed as he had talked about feeling. He was energized and involved in the session. He appears to be making some connections about causality with respect to feelings, expectations, needs and the difficulty in getting those needs met. CW:

7-10

Upon interview this morning Tim looked quite depressed. When asked about this he advised me that his dire predictions of the failure of his current temp job were coming true. He was not paid for last week, and it doesn't look like he will be paid for this week's work. It appears that this company is going to go under. We spent the entire session clarifying that this is happening not because there was something wrong with him, but because the company simply wasn't making it. He has a difficult time, by his own admission, in not withdrawing during times of stress such as these. I framed for him the fact that this was an opportunity for him to attempt to not regress by becoming isolated. He has in fact reached out to make contact with the manager of the local public radio station and has learned of the process by which jobs are listed in public radio throughout the country. He gives himself very little credit for this initiative. We also talked in some detail about the role of unpredictability and the feeling of anxiety. Tim appeared to be mildly depressed today. He is feeling frustrated and anxious at the present time.

The plan will be to emphasize the role that Tim's expectations and assumptions about himself have in his current feelings and his response to the increase in his stress engendered by the upcoming apparent loss of his temp job.

7-17

Tim was in a substantially brighter mood today than he was during the last two sessions. He attributes this improvement to taking to heart some of the conversations we are having regarding his assumptions about why the present job is not going to be working out; that being because of the company and not because of himself. We spent most of the session talking about the difficulty that Tim has with his expectation of rejection from other people. I identified to him that I believe that this was basically because he did not like himself, and that he did not meet his own standards. He does state that he was much more content in the Army in Vietnam when he was in charge of things, was not questioned, and was accepted as being a competent person. This is also the case when he was a "one man" newsroom at a local radio station. Tim was also challenged with respect to his resistance to making a demo tape that he might use for applying to radio station jobs, as well as not following up with possible employment opportunities in Minneapolis. He took these challenges well. We also talked about the nature of the relationship between us. At the end of the session he gave me a cigar. The reason for this was not exactly clear, but may be related to his efforts to pay me back in some way for the help he is getting. Tim has pulled himself out of the typical pattern of depression as a response to uncontrollable life events. he is appearing to be closer to taking more action with respect to seeking employment. He also is looking more willingly at his own assumptions about himself and his self respect/confidence/image. The present treatment plan will be continued with an emphasis on the above topics, particularly reasons why Tim may have difficulty accepting himself for whom he is. CW:

7-23

Tim continues to hang in his temp job, having been paid recently for the past two weeks. He continues to express some pessimism about the probability of this being a long term operation. We talked at some length about a recent event in which he had made an effort to obtain material so he could practice making a demonstration tape to be used for application for radio station jobs. Tim gave up after one small hurdle. We spent some time talking about why that may be and Tim concluded that it was because he really believed himself to be inferior and saw no point really in pretending that he could actually ever have a job or be successful in the radio business. Much of the session was spent in discussing and exploring the origins of his feelings of inferiority. Those feelings and impressions were gently but firmly disagreed with by the undersigned. I challenged him as to why it may be necessary for him to believe that he is inferior, perhaps because he will then have an excuse to not exert the choice that he actually has in his life. Tim left fairly abruptly in the session, stating that he needed to catch a bus.

Tim appears to be trying to come to grips with the fundamentals of his current dilemma, that being that he believes he is an inferior human being. This is difficult thing for him to talk about, but he hing in through most of the session before getting too anxious to stay. The plan is to continue with this therapeutic approach with Tim, recognizing that it may be a long term enterprise. CW:

7-31

Tim continues to be employed in a temp job, though he acknowledges that his most recent paycheck bounced. We spent much of the session talking about the possible origins of his feelings of being inferior, and also discussed the times in his life when he has felt competent. It is clear that Tim's feelings if being inadequate person and incompetent socially go back many years. During the military, however, he did have an extended period of time in which his personal feelings of confidence and competence were substantially improved. Since being discharged from the Army he acknowledges that he has had periodic times in which he felt more comfortable about his ability and felt less inferior. It is clear that it is impossible to logically convince Tim that he is not an inferior person. However, it appears that maintaining this belief is serving some function for Tim. Perhaps as he suggests, it may be an excuse to help him avoid dealing with the spectre of failure. CW:

1-6

Tim reports feeling more and more fed up with himself. He states that he cannot identify clearly what he wants to do, but is clearly increasingly dissatisfied with his own inertia. We spoke of different methods by which he could become more active, but voices little interest or commitment to any of these things, i.e. volunteering to community agencies. We also discussed a form that was completed by social services in support of his welfare application. Little change in Tim's behavior has been noted, though he reports feeling increasing internal conflict regarding his lack of action. Tim continues to manifest significant symptomatology of an avoidant personality disorder, and continues to maintain assumptions, previously identified, of inferiority and lack of self worth. CW:

1-14

Tim continues to manifest considerable frustration with his inaction. I've intentionally decided not to rush him, and this seems to have somewhat of a confounding effect on Tim. This session was characterized by several lengthy silences during which time Tim became increasingly frustrated and figidity. He acknowledges that he continues to be quite isolated from other people and appears to feel quite shameful about his unemployment and general station in life. The strategy of not pushing Tim is consonant with recommendations given by members of the treatment unit when this case was reviewed. Tim shows little progress or increase in symptoms. He is quite stable at the present time and exhibits a considerable amount of inertia. Countertransference issues are somewhat problematic at the present time but are being dealt by regular consultation with other clinical staff. The plan is to continue seeing Tim for support but to not push him into any specific action. This appears to be the best alternative in dealing with an individual who manifests considerable fear of rejection and considerable animosity towards authority figures. CW:

1-20

Today's session with Tim was characterized by considerable silence, as it was last week. Tim continues to obsess about his lack of activity. We talked at some length about demoralization, hopelessness, and the fact that life is what happens to you while you are planning for it. Tim acknowledges these things, but commits to no action to get himself out of his current rut Tim continues to show considerable social isolation and inertia. He voices frustration at his current situation, particularly going on welfare, but doesn't appear either motivated or continent enough to pursue alternate behavior. The plan is to continue supportive treatment with Tim, but continuing to avoid prescribing specific alternatives for his discomfort. CW:

1-27

Tim continues to express considerable frustration regarding his present station in life. He is annoyed that the people in the work readiness program are referring him to "practice" job interviews. He states that he would like to have some choice about this. He recognizes that he is caught in his own ambivalence not wanting to be told what to do, but not knowing what to do when left to his own devices. We spoke abut his symptomatology with respect to fear of rejection, as well as with respect to difficulty dealing with authority figures. All things considered, Tim continues to be essentially in the same existential dilemma which has been manifest for the past few months. He seemed frustrated with the therapy experience, as I am no longer giving him specific advice which he in turn fails to follow. He continues to obsess about his own lack of self worth/inferiority, but seems essentially unable to do even simple things to attach himself more to other people or to pursue job possibilities. The plan is to continue with an accepting atmosphere in therapy, but to avoid giving specific directions which Tim simply doesn't follow. CW:

2-16

A somewhat different approach in dealing with Tim was undertaken today. I told him that I believed that I had made a mistake in the past in trying to urge him to have hope, when in fact it appeared to be logically inconceivable that one person could make another person have hope. I told him that it would be more useful for me in dealing with him to undertake an observer role. I also advised him that it appears quite frequently that he is in an observer role, observing his own gradual demise. I also told him that I was quite curious as to what if would take for him to actually begin making some change rather than simply obsessing about it. This change in strategy appeared to be somewhat surprising to Tim, though he did not appear to be upseit by it. He appeared to be somewhat taken aback by my stated unwillingness to try and urge him to do better, when he in fact feels quite hopeless about this. Objectively, little has changed in his lifestyle over the past months.

3-2

Mr. Connelly continues to report feeling some ambivalence and confusion about what he should be doing. However, quite surprisingly, he has applied for three jobs over the past week. He is somewhat surprised at this, and continues to maintain a skeptical, pessimistic attitude toward the possibility of anything positive really happening. Additionally, and quite surprisingly, he began talking about his family of origin. In particular, he expressed considerable hatred and anti-authority feelings with respect to his father. Apparently his father has for years expected that Tim would be successful and has put pressure on him to do so. Tim does not appear to see the connection between this pressure and his reluctance to be successful. It appears that the strategy of observing Tim's gradual decline, as well as refusing to try to give him hope has been helpful in getting Tim in gear to do some things to take care of himself. It appears quite likely that this relationship to his father plays a major role in his difficulties at sustaining effort.

Much of the session was spent today in talking about life scripts, the hazards of being described as having great potential, and Tim's tendency to spend most of his time looking backward instead of looking ahead. Tim described what sounded like a slight anxiety attack which occurred sometime during the week. He continues to puzzle with many questions of why and I continue to be reluctant to get into the why questions, as they seem to presume and rational cause for behavior which is primarily emotionally based. He continues to make many self deprecating statements and continues to be quite aware that he has little tolerance for conflict. He also seems to be in the beginning phase of recognizing that he expects to fail, expects to be beaten in any argument and expects to be on a recurring cycle of getting his hopes up to be followed by rejection and failure. Tim is unclear about exactly he wants. He recognizes that he has low probablilty of successful employment. He does not appear to be as depressed as he initially was when seen two weeks ago. He denies any suicidal ideation or plan. The plan is to see Tim again in a week. At that time I will give him a treatment plan form to complete before the next session. CW:

3-18

Tim called with a very rare cancellation today. He did not reschedule. This is very unusual for Tim and may be related to a change in treatment strategy. If he does not call within two weeks, I will call him to discuss his continued therapy with him.

The Group
October 31
Week One

      I sat in a sparsely decorated room at the Post Trauma Stress
Clinic with three other men. It would be a seven week process trying
to deal with events of a war, which had left nightmares, flashbacks,
anger and depression. It got worse before it got better I was told. It was
Halloween. A good day to dig up the ghosts which had been haunting
us. I had come to Minneapolis many years ago to begin the journey off
to war and now perhaps this trip to Minneapolis would begin the
journey home.
      The group begins shortly after 8:30. Dr. Harry Russell is the
program director and psychologist. He introduces the program. I am
still not to sure about him. Dr. Edwin Smelker is the psychritrist. He is
funny but I feel some resentment toward him. Maybe it's because he is
a world war two veteran. Clay King is the social worker. He bugs me
but I don't know why as yet. Jean Miller is the occupational therapist.
She is nice and is also my coordinator. Kay Ryan is the nurse. She
talks about family issues. So far, she is okay, but it is to early to tell.
The patients are Dave the engineer who is also suicidal. He was a
recon man in the war. He is having marital problems and talks to
much. My first impression is that I don't like the guy. David is heavily
drugged or something and says very little. He was in the airborne.
Mike was a medic in the war. He is nervous and makes me nervous.
Art was a grunt and is now a biker. He is the strong silent type. Then
there is me.
After a short break, some guy talks to us about benefits and education
and employment and so forth. He will be seeing us again individually,
perhaps. At noon we get a bag lunch with mystery meat sandwiches.
We sat around and listened as Dave talked nonstop about the war.
About 1pm we go to occupational therapy. We cut out pictures from
old magazines to show how we feel about our life and goals at the
current time. David hates the exercise and doesn't take part. We wrap
up around 2:30 for the first day and head home. I don't know if this
program will help a thing but I will try it out for awhile.

Tuesday:

We are shown a film about a stress program in California. We also have a new group member. Dan was a medic in the navy and was attached to the Marines. His whiney voice drives me up the wall. At the end of the movie, Dave and Dan start crying. Mike and myself are uneasy with this display of emotion and walk out of the room.
About 10 we start talking about our war experiences in group. Dave is the most vocal. He suffers from guilt over the deaths of two squad members and for some reason wants to go into the woods and kill people. Dave and Mike are at odds with some type of personality conflict. Later in OT we draw a life line. Mike seems to have a lot of personal problems with his wife, home, kids and job. Dan seems to be screwed up with his family life too.

Friday:

I have lost a couple of days here and there. I was going to be faithful to this journal but am being half assed as usual. I have been overwhelmed and my memory is jammed. What happened yesterday? I can't really remember. I wondered if I was aware of my guilt feelings about the war. Was it guilt of who I was, rather than what I did or didn't do? Was I in touch with the meaning events had on me? Was it guilt over my curiosity in the face of death and the sense I had been an onlooker? Did I need to confess? Was the guilt an outgrowth of fear? Or did guilt increase fear. Was it guilt over having suffered less than others? I had been an onlooker in war and was still doing it to this day. I stood back from involvement. I wanted to become less of an onlooker in life but was afraid I would break down like in the war. There was stress involving experiences with sick, wounded, dying and dead soldiers and civilians. I do think I was profiecent at times.

Monday:

We have an education session about PTSD and I have an individual meeting with Jean Miller. Not much is discussed. In OT we make a map of where we were stationed. It was kind of an easy day but most of us feel numb. I sat next to a guy who was eating carrots on the bus ride today. Weird!

Tuesday:

Cease Fire, a movie about a crazed vet starring Don Johnson, is shown. I am not to impressed with the movie myself. It is the same old stuff. Boring. In group we discuss what I did in the war. I couldn't read a story I had writted about my experiences but I did show some pictures I had from the war to the group. I told the group I was angry but didn't know why. I trembled as I slapped my leg with my hand, tears rolling down my cheeks. "Hey man why do you feel guilty when you were trying to save people," Art asked, "while I was trying to kill people. I am the one with guilt."
Mike was a medic. He had been wounded in a firelight and pinned down for eight hours. He couldn't move after being hit by a grenade. It had been so surreal a feeling to him. He was a medic and couldn't do anything for the guys being shot-up all around him. David screams, "For all anyone cares we might as well all be dead. I wondered why I had gotten myself into this shit.
In Ot we paint pictures. Mine is looking at war from a distance. A face one half light the other dark. I am upset. Damn, I don't understand why.

Week Three
Monday:

I am extremely nervous. I didn't want to come today. I will be staying at a place called Heilman House near the Veterans Home. I wonder if it was named after the beer. It is a place for homeless veterans. Five to six guys to a room. It reminds me of the barracks in Germany. Old, dark and hot.

I really don't want to stay here very much. Art didn't show today. I don't think he will come back. Heilman House or as I have renamed it Hell House sucks. It is going to be a long fucking week. Why did I get myself into this shit. I just want to be happy.

Tuesday:

We see the movie Full Metal Jacket. In group David tells about an officer who died in an ambush. David cared for the guy and expressed anger about how the man's body was treated with no respect and was dragged in the mud. David also talked about a friend named Willie who was killed. His body stripped and castrated. He still has a recurring nightmare about the incident. It is the first time David has really opened ip. He says he feels exhausted. I think we all do. Mike really is jumpy today. He needs a job and his problem with his wife is not getting better(whatever that is).
Art didn't show again today. I am not focused on war stuff.
I hate Hell House and am worried about my economic situation. Oh shit! I don't know if this program is really worth it.

Wednesday:

First snow storm of the season. Art is missing for a third day. I don't know if he is coming back. I am depressed. In group, David talks about being in a porn movie at age 16 after he ran away from home to LA. Again more war stories. I sit silent in the corner. I don't see any theraputic value in this bullshit. In OT, we draw pictures about our view of ourselves. Mine view is negative as usual. I want to go home.

Thursday:

Art returned after being sick with a cold for a few days. We are given a lecture on fear along with a film. Dan says we owe our enemies an apology. There is going to be a lot of down time today for some reason. Mike seems in a better mood today while Dave hasn't talked much all this week. I feel tense. Back at Hell House with the boys on the edge. Damn, I know if this place doesn't motivate me, I don't know what will.

Friday:

Art didn't show today. We see a movie about depression. Dr. Smelker leads group. Mike seems in better spirits. While David seems to be really spaced out by his medication. Dave is laid back. I feel like a bundle of depressed nerves. But Dan has finally stopped his whining episodes.

Week Four:

David is late today while Mike is stuck in traffic but everyone seems in a good mood. Dave and his wife are meeting with Kay Ryan and he seems more distant and withdrawn. Dan says he is scared but seems to be getting more into things. I don't know what I feel. Another discussion about depression. I am a professional depressant. At individual therapy with Jean Miller, I explain my need to worry about my economic situation. I am on welfare with no hope in sight. I need a job and I hate living in Hell House. I don't think anyone understands where I am coming from anymore. Jean wants me to contact my family about the PTSD program or call one of the other guys in the PTSD program or to get in touch with an old high school buddy who is interested in starting a veterans group. I just don't want to bother people. Jean is also pushing me or harassing me about getting out and seeing the city. I hate the city. I just want to be off in some small town stuck in an apartment. It is a safe rut to be in and it is comfortable and it would be my choice not someone elses. Other people don't know what is best for me. Besides the city is enemy territory and I don't venture out in an unsecure area without backup or self protection—like the handgun I keep hidden in my backpack.

Tuesday:

We see a movie called Anderson Platoon. It is the same unit Mike was with and was film in the same area he was stationed during the war. The movie was okay. I have some uneasy feelings when they show wounded people. In group we focus a lot on Art. He tells about a friend who was killed and how he has always wanted to go see the parents of the man and tell them how their son died. He now feels he has the nerve to do it. Dr. Smelker says talking with the parents will

give the death of Art's friend some sense of meaning. Art also talks about being a funeral color guard for a man from his home town. He had a tough time dealing with the experience and said the mother of the dead soldier refused to accept the American flag. Art seems to be opening up while I close down. I can't relate to these guys. Dave gets kind of emotional. I sense a lot of bitter feelings in that man. He is scary. Mike is hyper and I don't know what is eating him and he doesn't know either. Dan begins whining again when he tells a story and it just drives me nuts. David is spaced out as usual. He says JFK's death really means or feels something to him now before it didn't mean a thing. It hit home like a rocket, he said. I am uncomfortable and sick of talking and listenting to stories about the war. Mike asks if I feel guilt over not being in a combat unit. Maybe? Of course.
In OT we make masks. Mine is the Lone Ranger. Mike is good at art and his mask looks professional. Dan has a lump of something for a mask. Dave has a black faced death mask. David and Art are not really into the project but seem to be developing something in their words it is a lot of bullshit.

Wednesday:

The end of week four and I still am nervous. I dread going to group. I may be cornered on my war experiences. I am prepared to read some stuff I have written while killing time at Hell House. Kay Ryan talks about social isolation. I know a lot about the subject. I don't over any feedback and she says I am a hard case. Mike went to get medical assistance for his wife and missed group. We talk about the jobs we have held and the relationship of the war and the ability to stay employed. David tells about his many jobs. His biggest fear about work is relating well with other people Once he was a bus driver for the city. He got upset one day with the people on the bus. So he parked the vehicle and walked away from the job leaving the passengers stranded. We all have a common thread dealing with other people and the anger and anxiety it causes with work. In Ot, we continue mask making. We will have four days of freedom because of the Thanksgiving holiday. I am thankful to get out of here.

Week Five
Monday:

I feel guilty about coming today. I feel that I should be out in the mainstream as a productive and functioning person in the real work world. I should be looking for a job to pay my bills. I can't afford to pay anything to anyone. I don't know what to do. I guess I will apply for social services. I need some advice. Dr. Smelker says I am rathering boring. We get a lecture on guilt and shame today. The guilt has to do with the fact we feel good for not getting killed, others did. Mike expresses feelings of not doing enough. Shame. I am not any good and I never was. I still am confused on the guilt issue. I am not sure if or what I am guilty about. Is it survivor guilt? I have a cold and feel uncomfortable and overwhelmed by everything. In individual therapy, Jean says I appear to be sadder today but more calm and not as nervous. She says it looks as if I could cry and that's exactly how I do feel. I do let a few tears out as I discuss how lonely I feel. Jean wants me to express those feelings in group and to ask for help in being less isolated. I don't know. In OT,we draw pictures about how we feel and see ourselves as group members. Dan draws the spokes of a wheel. He is really out of it today and down on himself. I draw a goofy picture of a flower, balloons and bugs. Art draws six guys in a boat, adrift. David draws different types of faces while Mike draws us as pieces of a puzzle and Dave draws a pair of dice. We represent the six black spots. Dan says he doesn't belong in group, and doesn't think the war is the root of his problems. Dr. Smelker wants to hear more from me. Dave and Mike seem more upbeat. I still feel like shit as I return for another evening at Hell House.

Tuesday:

It's 6am. I am sitting here in Hell House and I want to leave. This is the strongest urge yet to run.
The movie today is Medal of Honor Rag. It is about a guy who wins the medal of honor, has PTSD, and gets killed robbing a store. It is based on a true story. David is very silent today. Dave is also not very talkative and is very cool and non- feeling when he does say something. He talks about the war and can't remember the names of friends killed in action. Mike says he is proud of winning the bronze star and purple heart but nobody really cares or cared after he returned

home. He worked at his peak during the war and figured he was going to die anyway. He had a spiritual experience but can't reason why he has trouble working at that peak effort now days or if he ever can again. Mike tells of his recurring dream about dying. Art says he has a similar dream of being shot and tells of being ambushed and how an enemy soldier pointed a gun at him but it didn't fire. There was no bullet in the chamber. He took a shot at the enemy the next day but he didn't know if it was the say guy. He feels guilty about the whole incident. Art says the PTSD program won't make any difference and tells about the time a guy was going to shoot him at a local bar. He feels he gets into dangerous situations in order to have someone kill him. I am asked if I have ever had feelings of killing anyone. The only thing I have ever killed is a case of beer, I say.

In OT, we make stuff from clay representing our strength or goals we bring to group. Dan makes a heart and brain. Art has a goal of building a cabin in the woods. David makes little clay figures representing his wife and kids. Dave makes a broken family and I make the symbols for truth and justice. Mike's not in OT today he had to go sign some papers because he might be evicted from his home. The group clay project results in a ball, bat, glove and home plate. Art makes a clay grenade. Dave a shell and knife. I make an archway with a figure of a man looking to get into the game or home. Who the hell knows what it means?

Wednesday:

I have arrived late today and it makes me mad. Art didn't show today. I feel things have been hard for him and he doesn't feel the program will change anything in his life. I kind of agree with his line of thought. After the program, we think we will be back into the same old shit. Kay Ryan has a discussion about boundaries and beliefs. Most of the other guys list stuff like love, family and religion. I have nothing. No concrete belief system that I can identify. She talks about family and relationships. I can't relate to the others in that respect. Kay goes over some family charts she has made. She relates how I have cut myself off from everybody in my family. We run out of time. I feel lonely and sad about being so cut off from other people. The central issue bothering all of us is discussed in group. The feat that keeps us from functioning in society like we functioned during the war. Why can't we perform like we did over there in everyday life? How do we overcome that fear which is always there inhibiting us from doing anything with our lives. There will be no answers today. Dr. Russell keeps repeating the theme. Why in a place where you would expect a person to lose control did you function and then in the relative safety of normal everyday life we just can't seem to get with the flow of things. We have to work on the issue of fear. In OT we draw pictures. One of a depressing thought and one positive dream. Dan draws a guy trapped on an island reaching for a ladder from the sky(hope), and draws an apple tree for a positive dream. David draws snow as depressing and a beach scene as a positive. Dave draws a pit and a pendulum and a farm for his positive dream. Mike draws a forest at night and a college degree as a goal. I draw a guy sitting on the dock of the bay to represent loneliness and a picture of an award for some type of recognition of accomplishment. I feel so out of place.

Thursday:

Trust is the topic of this morning's discussion by Dr. Russell. Do we trust people? Why don't we trust people? Do we have friends? The focus is mainly on the guys with wives and whether they trust each other. I am not with the discussion today for some reason. We are shown another boring war movie and a film on evil. Do we feel we are evil or killers because of our wartime experiences? How do we see ourselves? Dr. Russell wants Art to open up more. Art says he takes the war stuff home with him and it has increased his depression. David adds he use to do that but now is more able to leave the war stuff ouside the home except during certain moods. Mike still gets nervous and paranoid when people visit or if he gets a phone call. He is afraid to answer the phone or go get the mail from his front porch. He tells us he now has a small home improvement job. He is glad but says he doesn't feel that way. Dan and his wife met with Dr. Russell and says he feels much better today. He knows is is overly emotional. I go and see a vocational psychologist. He asks about my job history and so forth. I don't know if it will go anywhere. I will have another appointment next week. There's something strange. I feel good or up after seeing the guy. I don't know why. I have to suppress the feeling as I walk back to Hell House.

Friday:

Dr. Smelker takes us to the OT room for a session on developmental psych. We draw life lines from age five to age 20 or until we went to war and then outline the significant events of those years both good and bad. David and Dan had rough childhoods. Their parents died or they were abandoned and so forth. Dave talks about farm life in North Dakota and how hard the work was but he didn't know any different. Mike had a fairly stable boring childhood. David, Dan and Mike all joined the service at 17. Art says he was a trouble maker in school so he joined the Army. I tell a lie and say I had a normal childhood in small town USA. It seems like most of us were set up for stress producing things to come in the war.

Week Six
Monday:

Dr. Smelker begins a discussion and review of PTSD and physical symptoms. We then trail off into a talk on loss friends, morals and self. Have we ever really mourned the losses or do we even know how to morn? I tell Jean, in a session, I really feel lonely and uncomfortable. She says I appear less nervous and that I need to continue to grow after the seven week program. I hope I can do so. OT is difficult today for Art and myself. We have to make something which indicates who we rely on for support now and in the future. It mainly deals with relationships. We all feel alone. I can't make any future decisions and neither can Art. We just react. I feel overwhelmed and want to cry.

Tuesday:

I come in late as the guys are watching the movie Dear America. The movie seems to touch more emotions in most of us except Dave. I kind of feel like crying. Dan is crying as usual while Mike and Art say the movie moved them. Mike says the movie really stirred some emotions but he says he only remembers certain things about the war such as RandR and three battles, One battle he was pinned down. He tried to drag this wounded offier to safety but couldn't. The officer was dying and talking about his family. Mike couldn't do anything and wishes the guy would die. Mike doesn't understand. He got a medal for the firefight but didn't help the officer. He still has a hang-up about receiving the medal. Art says the movie stirred up feelings. He says he was a sucker and has no faith in this country or the flag. There's nothing a person can do. The war happened and we have to live with it. He talks about being a rebel as a biker, of taking drugs and drinking. He just wants to be left alone. He says he will never have kids, or a home, or a steady job, or the American Dream. He doesn't really want it. I don't either.

I think along the same line. I died years ago and went into isolation. I see no future and no way out except death. I am pissed off that I am in this situation. Mike says the time since the war could have meant something but they don't mean a thing. In OT we draw the strengths we see in each other. Art is seen as having mechanical abilities and a strong sense of free spririt. David is seen as guy with a sense of humor and a strong heart but very confused. Dave is analytical, mechanical and a good provider but something is haunting him. We see Mike as creative. Dan as a good hearted person with compassion for all. I am seen as able to communicate ideas. Art draws an army helmet on a radio to represent me. David says he is having sleep problems and awoke pushing his wife out of bed. Dan is having nighmares about problems he has trying to raise a young daughter.

Wednesday:

David keeps repeating the same stories about the war and relates then to phobias he now has about going out of the house into crowds. He would rather stay inside. We don't talk about war issues much today. I read something I have written about fear but there is no follow up discussion. Mike is distant and leaves at noon to do some work. In OT we draw and paint a Christmas tree. I leave early to talk with the vocational shrink. I am question by an intern about problems I have had in recent work relationships and other conflicts. I will see th guy again next week but I am not optimistic about the whole thing.

Thursday:

A discussion on the Hierach of Needs by Abraham Maslow. David and Mike not in group today. Survival, safety, love, self esteem, self actualization. We need this things. Veterans with PTSD are stuck in survival and safety mode. Self actualiztion is when we accept ourselves. It is slow today with not much going on. Lunch is long and boring with the usual mystery meat. After lunch two chemical dependency counselors talk about chemicals and PTSD. The two counselors are going to school to become CD workers. They tell their stories about war and PTSD. The thing that bothers me most is their point of view. They take pride in going to war. We deserve more and war was right. I can't accept their bullshit. Art likes the CD talk. Dave said it depressed him. The two guys brought up a couple things he had forgot which triggered some memories. The CD guys did make one good point. We veterans don't treat each other very well. If you weren't an airborne ranger killing people you are made to feel guilty for not doing your duty. We were all in the same boat but we never acknowledge it. One week left of this group. A lot of waiting. Waiting sums up my existence.
I am always waiting. I am unable to go forward with my miserable life.

Week Seven
Monday:

Well it's here. Week seven. David is going to the hospital for an interview to get into another group program. He say he feels good about it. Mike is nervous as hell. Dan is worried about money issues but is not totally bummed out. We are given a review of PTSD by Dr. Russell. It will always be part of us. But we can learn to deal with it. However, some event might trigger something off in the future and we will have to come back for a tune up. Thinking and feeling. Fear and anger. Let's hope we don't have to come back to often. I meet with Jean. What will I do next. Go to the Day Hospital program with David? No, I don't think so. I want to wait out the winter and will keep in contact with Jean once a week for awhile. I am scared of the future and want to keep going forward. Jean says people really care about me. A tear comes to my eye. It's hard to accept that somebody really cares about Tim Connelly. In OT we make clay models of gifts for each other. I again have an appointment with the vocational counselor to go over some tests. The tests will tell me what jobs I can best do. Yeah sure. Dave discussed an incident during the war while we were making our clay models. He found a chain at home with two bullets on it. One from a M-16, the other from an AK-47. He had shot at an enemy soldier but his rifle jammed. The enemy soldier was going to fire at Dave but didn't because another guy with Dave shot and killed the enemy. The bullet meant for Dave was still in the enemy soldier's rifle chamber. He made a chain to remind himself how close death was and can be.

Tuesday:

We see our final movie. It is about a war memorial. A tear even came to my eye but I don't know why. Perhaps it was when I saw the mothers of dead soldiers crying over lives thrown away for nothing. Mike is worried about the future after group. He has all these things he wants to do but what if everything just remains the same. I think it's tough to plan ahead any length of time and you usually just end up being disappointed anyway. Mike didn't like the patriotic tone of the movie and says it's hard to be part of a brotherhood of veterans. I agree. David is angered over having to fight for benefits from the VA all the time. Art says a memorial is a good thing from veterans to remember the dead. I don't know. I feel we ought to accept we lost the war and help the living. It seems the dead are all over with honor. We honor the dead soldiers but what about all the dead civilians? What about all the guys who have died since the war? There is a long period of silence. Art and Dave say they want to be happy but how do they achieve that feeling.
We make billboard in OT to portray ourselves. David seems more up the past couple of days. He draws a Coke and Dance sign back in the 1960's cruising stuff. I draw a billboard that says space for rent. Mike draws a war scene which says everyone suffers in war. Dave draws the same thing as me. Art draws a motorcycle and boat while Dan draws a wounded man and a medic helping him. Mike says he will take me to a local veterans meeting but I have the feeling I am invading his space and don't feel comfortable. I back off. I feel sorry later as I sit on my bunk in Hell House.
I should have gone with Mike. I don't know what is wrong with me.

Wednesday:

We have a talk about what we can do in our spare time to relax or activites to pursue in the off hours to enhance ourselves. In group we discuss how we feel the group has been. David says he feels good about being in the program and it has helped him to make the decision to go to Day Hospital for more treatment. I say the program has been positive but maybe has only scratched the surface. I am told the program is only the beginning. I have to talk with more people. Jean says veterans in isolation seem to have the most problems adjusting. Dave says he is happier and it seems the little things don't bother him as much as they did before. He is excited to bet back to work and still has hope he can keep the family together some way or another. Art says the program has helped him recognize some problems and he kind of wishes he had stable employment and a stable life but isn't worried about the future. Dan says he is greatful for the program and goes off into his flowery bullshit. He hopes to get back to work and keep the family together and worry less. In OT we draw pictures on how we feel today. A layer of feelings compared to what we did seven weeks ago. The pictures this time exhibit more hope and positive feelings. I hope it can continue.

Thursday:

It's here. The last day of group. Art didn't show because he says his care won't start. It felt incomplete without him. Kay Ryan reviewed family systems and everyone agreed the family stuff was good and it helped up get to know each other better had have some shared experiences and showed up where we came from. We meet for a final time and give our feedback which is basicly that the program is a positive step. Dr.Russell gives us feedback. He says Dan should be less serious. Mike should worry less. Dave should learn to relax. David should open up more to people. He say he thought I would not make it and would have runaway the first week but I fooled him. The group agrees to meet on Tuesdays but I won't be able to make it or I don't want to make it. We are served some cake and ice cream and Dr. Russell plays his guitar. It's time for me to leave. I shake hands with everyone and take by backpack and walk out the door. A few hours later reality has set in. I am back on my bunk in the same old trap. The post program high has lasted a whole two hours. Oh shit! Now what?

Dr Zigfrids is the director of the county crisis center and a recognized expert on suicide.
The purpose of the conference is to review with Dr. Zigfrids his report on some some specific cases and to go over recommendations for program improvement.

Dr. Zigfrids: "I will summarize the findings of my review of the cases. All the patients were at high risk for suicide and violence. All were similar with regard to age, background and chronicity. The three patients who died were in significantly disturbed marital relationships with threats of imminent divorce. The precipitant for the final event was the threat of divorce. In one case the split of family may have prevented the children, who knew their father had a gun hidden in his car, from letting anyone know. The man used this weapon in his suicide. Finally, these patients viewed the hospital as a sanctuary, and had repeated and sometimes lengthy hospitalizations."

"I find no evidence of clinical mismanagement of any of these veterans but on the other hand, there are important issues which need to be examined. I lack the expertise in PTSD but some of these problems are commonly encountered in a variety of treatment settings."

The hospital as sanctuary. Is it regressive? Dr. Zigfrids had questions about this, especially the fostering of regression by lengthy hospitalizations.

Dr. Zigfrids: "I wonder too if lengthy hospitalization is compatible with repeated passes."(The hospital staff has noted in other meetings the lack of weekend programming and the concomitant wish to say "yes" to pass requests. "I also have reservations about the contract promising not to commit suicide, as there may be no significant clinical advantage to such a maneuver, although it may be helpful legally." I wonder if there are other formal methods of assessing suicide potential in addition to the rating scale used by the nursing staff. A more formal method by the doctor might be in order. However, a suicide remains unpredictable no matter what the scale or method. And the patients in question had multiple assessments."

What about the PTSD group culture? Does the clustering of PTSD patients, especially those with chronic courses, helpful or harmful?

Harm may result from reinforcement of symptoms and destructive attitudes, but group does provide support. Who provides positive role models in the culture/groups other than the therapists?

Social Worker Mike Green: "In the planning for the Here and Now group, outpatients are to be included for that reason."

Dr. Russell: "I have pointed out many times that the outpatient program has many clients who are doing well."

Dr. Dean: "Is there some way in which these better functioning patients could be integrated into the group program, especially with inpatients?"

There remains much disagreement among the staff about clustering, and whether this prevents reintegrating these patients into the community. The patients virtually insist on it, and indeed this has been a primary demand of theirs. There is little data on which to base such a tactic. Further, no other patients, save for CD clients are segregated. However the PTSD group is marked by uncommon commonality.

There is a phenomenon of resistance. There is a reluctance of PTSD patients on inpatient to deal with anything except what their concepts of PTSD encompass. They actively resist efforts at enrolling in CD treatment, for example, and often resist attending other parts of the program, even when seemingly relevant such as grief and loss group and a group on cognitive aspects of depression.

Dr Smelker: "I object to the term resistance. Such maneuvers could be more profitably thought of as survival mechanisms."

Dr. Dean: "It seems to me that such defenses are self destructive." "Certainly withdrawal and isolation are not survival mechanisms and clearly not in combat were group support and cooperation must be present. Perhaps these maneuvers should be seen as self destructive and stemming from the immense guilt guilt experienced by many."

It seems to be the opinion of the PTSD staff that CD issues are secondary and that the confrontational approach used by many groups could not be tolerated by most patients with PTSD. Inpatient staff notes that a number of chronic PTSD patients have current and significant CD problems but more needs to be done to directly address the issue.

Dr Dean: " I would like to point out one current inpatient who is using amphetamines and methamphetamines and who is on 15 years probation for dealing, but this was not addressed or even mentioned in the otherwise copious PTSD notes." "Can this patient, and another currently using alcohol and marijuana while in intensive outpatient therapy, be effectively treated for PTSD while using?"

Dr. Murray: "I wonder whether the deaths would have occurred had not their CD problems been so prominent."

Dr. Zigfrids: "We have no way of knowing that, and certainly other issues especially marital dysfunction were present nonetheless."

Dr. Dean: "Patients in the outpatient group must be willing to maintain strict sobriety during the entire treatment program. If this requirement is presently in place it is not being observed in the cases seen by the inpatient staff. Their histories indicate an ongoing pattern of chemical abuse while in the PTSD program while in out patient treatment. And as one might expect, there is usually strong opposition to random urine screening in the hospital."

Dr Dean: "I wonder if the staff has been intimidated by threats of suicide, violence and withdrawal from the program. If the staff is over fearful of suicide, then other issues, especially the treatment of CD will be put aside. I wonder if we in fact are enabling patients in their use of street drugs and perhaps psychotic drugs as well."

Dr Zigfirds: "The staff cannot focus on suicide exclusively, as first, it is not predictable, and second, the opportunities exist everywhere, even in the hospital. Naturally, one takes precautions, but if prevention of suicide is the primary focus, little else can be accomplished."

Dr Russell: "The PTSD outpatient program has had one suicide in 10 years."

Dr Dewy: "At some point therapists have to move on from a sympathetic approach to other goals. I work in grief and loss and the present difficulties with PTSD. At some point, one considers saying enough, now what are you going to do about it?"

Dr. Dean: "I wonder if more active family intervention might have forestalled tragedy."

Dr Russell: The outpatient PTSD program has a greatly expanded and more intensive family therapy approach."

Dr. Yang: "I wonder if providing a specific program for PTSD would be helpful. The PTSD patient virtually relates everything in his or her life is caused by PTSD and unless the patient perceives you are dealing directly with PTSD he or she often rejects the effort. The patient seems to be caught in the middle of two conflicting philosophies of treatment, that is, between the PTSD staff approach and that of inpatient."

Dr. Zigfrids: "The concept of the disorder and treatment philosophies drive any program, especially when hard data is lacking."

Dr. Dill: "I have noticed patients respond angrily if inpatient staff begin to push re-participation in CD or other program functions. They claim the staff is rejecting then and doesn't understand PTSD. There is a widespread feeling among inpatient staff that this response is reinforced by The PTSD staff, and once again places the patient squarely in the middle of the conflict."

Dr. Dean: "This kind of split may result in a "good-guy, bad-guy" dichotomy with the PTSD staff in the good-guy role, and the inpatient staff playing the heavy. This is a pattern without question. No doubt patients exploit the split, probably worsening it."

Dr. Zigfrids: "Hospitalization should be used only when there is no alternative, or when protection is needed. Often remarkable improvement is seen within hours of admission."

Dr. Yang: "I feel that compensation is a significant issue for many patients. There's a strong disincentive to brief hospitalization in the form of the 21 day rule, giving veterans an increase to 100% if hospitalization lasts over 21 days. This fact is sometimes mentioned by patients asking for a greater length of stay."

Dr. Dean: "Too often inpatient staff is left wondering what the purpose of admission might be and what the therapist is hoping to accomplish. If staff goals are vague, then the patient will fill the vacuum with his or her goals whether they seem reasonable to staff or not."

Dr. Zigfrids: I recommend a consistent staff person perhaps the psychiatrist to monitor and coordinate planning."

Dr. Dewy: "I think thought should be given to triaging these patients. Once it becomes evident that therapy is not progressing and that it serves only as friendship and general support, those tasks should be taken on by people other than mental health professionals."

Dr. Magraw: "The Vietnam war resulted in divisiveness among the staff but those wounds are largely healed. Nevertheless, the staff remains divided and not only inpatient and PTSD but within the inpatient staff itself. We cannot continue to have separate programs and separate approaches."

Dr Dean:" Several of our patients now have sons and daughters in the Middle-East. One patient has already said he'd rather have his son dead that return with PTSD! I have said before that our present patients may quickly find themselves displaced as their war will not be the most recent major war, and concerns of the veterans of 30 years ago will be supplanted by planning and concerns over our new casualties. This will be especially difficult for the Vietnam veterans as they now feel they are getting the recognition they have deserved. Some staff have stated that these patients are already in the process of defending their territory. No doubt some are having memories further stirred by the current fighting. How will the present patients be of help to the incoming, or will they indeed inadvertently damage the new casualty by helping to foster a cynical, mistrusting attitude of the VA's PTSD program."

The Psychotherapy of Vietnam Veterans

In talking about the psychotherapy of the Vietnam veteran, I would like to report what I think I have learned from my patients. This will be my clinical impression and should not be confused either with basic facts or a "how to manual.' In the middle 1970's I arrived at a beginning awareness of PTSD when I happened to see a half dozen or a dozen veterans who reported the same symptoms, e.g. fatigue, anger with constricted affect, nightmares, insomnia, isolation, etc. These veterans were quite different in their personalities and backgrounds. Only their service in Vietnam was similar and could explain the peculiar constellation of symptoms. Since that time I have seen hundreds of vets with this syndrome in the setting of the hospital and mental health clinic. I have worked with them in groups and in individual psychotherapy. Some have been with me in treatment for up to ten years. I often wondered if I could treat one of these veterans for longer than a decade. So far I have not had to face that possibility. As a group, I find these patients lively, interesting, and committed to change. They require shift in the usual position of the therapist. The role of the expert amuses then or worse, invites criticism. The word criticism tends to take on a new meaning in their hands and usually involves a string of expletives of easily recognized origin and vocabulary choice. The concept of calculated risk in case management needs to be markedly broadened when assessing dangerousness to self and others. There are moments that leave the therapist intolerably anxious. Indeed the therapist experiences many symptoms that are similar to PTSD. The strengths of the patient to survive must always be remembered and do offer some comfort in the middle of the night when one is wondering if the patient is holding a gun to his or someone else's head. Established rapport with these patients is more difficult and takes longer than the usual patient. Although they have a commitment to change and to get help, the patient must deal with his hard earned distrust of others. Remember the cause of PTSD comes from the environment, which has threatened the very existence of the individual. Because the vet's orientation is to explain all difficulties on external causes the very nature of psychotherapy is 1. frustrating, 2. confusing, and 3. frightening. 1. Frustrating because therapy introduces new complexities and possibilities when the patient wants to cling to his oversimplified explanation and solution to the problem so that he can have closure, which reduces his anxiety. 2. Confusing because the therapist tends to identify with the left-brain world in which the patient feels very uncomfortable. 3. Frightening because the language and thought of the therapist represent a part of the world that the patient has come to fear.

The veteran is poorly equipped to handle either emotions of ideas. Both of these areas of functioning have been largely sacrificed for the purpose of survival and consequently are avoided. In the crisis situation emotions have no survival value with the exception of anger, which can be helpful by providing self- confidence and motivation to take action. Otherwise the individual has no choice to shove aside any feelings into the unconscious. In the parlance of PTSD the patient becomes numb and is unaware of feelings. An example of how this state develops can be seen in the soldier who looses a friend in war. If he mourns he cannot attend to the threats around him and react to them effectively. However, he is able to transpose mourning into anger, which he can use for action in the service of revenge. If he can do bad things to the enemy who killed his friend he can correct or make right his friend's death.

The concepts of right and left brain functions have been useful to me in helping the veteran understand what he goes through in everyday life a well a his experience in war. The idea that the two hemispheres of the brain perform different functions comes from the research done on the so call split brain patients. In the 1960's doctors in California operated on severe seizure patients who were immobilized by their repeated and incapacitating seizures. They severed the neural connections between the two hemispheres called the corpus callosum. Through their research it became clear that the human has two ways of interpreting the world. The left-brain thinks in the way that we ordinarily identify with. It is the thinking of logic linear time, reading, writing, etc. In other words, it is the thinking of the civilized world with which we identify in everyday life. It functions much like a computer, using bits of information in the proper order to arrive at a solution. It is a serial process. Ordinarily we are unaware that we have another way of understanding reality. The other way is the thinking if the right brain which constructs a world around us providing all its components and their relationships to each other. This function makes it possible to distinguish a thousand faces and remember them. It provides instant recognition of complicated scenes and picks out any irregularities. It is a world of form, emotions, bodily sensations, and perceptions. All of these parts of our personality are organized under this function. For instance, the right brain gives us quick and easy solutions in recognizing right or left hands in pictures while the left brain requires a time consuming process of point by point comparisons of details of pictures to arrive at a solution. The experiences of war were right brain experiences. The quick global analysis of the environment required that the right brain functions be dominant, e.g. being able to look at a jungle scene with its bewildering array of foliage and pick out the enemy or the "wrong" part of the scene. Since the 1950's military training has become efficient in changing the individual for this life of extreme crisis and trauma. Now the first thing the serviceman hears when he gets to basic training is the constant repetition of the idea "don't think, you are not paid to think, you are paid to react," etc. This technique begins the process of undermining the dominance of the left-brain. There is the added application that the left-brain is dangerous and needs to be avoided. The left-brain can get you killed. If you think, you are dead. There is an important truth behind this training, which is that the central nervous system needs to be altered and retrained to handle incoming stimuli in a different way. The perception of anything outside of ourselves comes first to the brain stem where the process of alerting the brain is set in motion. The next center at which the stimuli arrives is the limbic system, which is part of our primitive brain and is shared by all mammals. It coordinates the basic survival responses such as the fight-flight reflex, which prepares the animal and the human for action. The limbic system needs to be trained in the human to route the stimuli to action areas of the brain and not send the information to the cerebral cortex where precious time will be used to organize a more elaborate response typical of the human. This retraining produces a considerable faster reaction time by several milliseconds. This bit of time is often the difference between life and death in war. Training only started the change toward more efficient reactions but more was needed after the soldier arrived in Vietnam. It seems to have taken about three to six weeks to adapt to the situation so that reaction time was reduced to acceptable times. This idea comes from the reports of my patients and their response to the "new guys." It was not until after the three to six week period that they began to trust the new man. During the year in Vietnam it was seldom that the dominance of the right brain was challenged. Rarely was a need for left-brain processes needed – a letter from home or a brief action report. It was a world of little thinking, constricted affect, constant alertness, and struggle against sleep. One of the remarkable aspects of the Vietnam experience was the unique time sense that was common to the soldiers. Because Vietnam was essentially a "right brain" experience the sense of time was not linear. The concept of future and past were ignored and remained unused. The individual lived in the present and in moments of relative calm, fantasized only briefly about returning home. These fantasies did not have a real quality with any substance. Rather the person thought in terms of buying a care or visiting a hamburger joint. The quality of time took on two varieties: 1. There was the present time during which the individual was waiting for something to happen, and the happening was always anticipated as something life threatening or "bad." The outcome was seen as the situation getting worse. The style of thought was part of the military training of anticipating the worst scenario and preparing for it. And 2. The other quality of time occurred when there was combat action. This was experienced as confusing, frightening, and sometimes overwhelming. Time seemed to stand still while incredibly bizarre situations were reacted to and solved almost automatically. These two states of consciousness although quite different in character both took place in present time. They were remarkably similar to the two mammalian self-preservation reflexes with their know neurological structures. The more human or cortical aspects of these reactions could probably be thought of in terms of depression and withdrawal during the waiting periods and anxiety during the moments of actual combat. It is fascinating to watch these patients shift from one state of consciousness to another. They display the usual state one sees during ordinary conversation when they attempt to communicate directly with the therapist on his ground, namely with left brain language. Soon they will become fatigued or upset with this chore and shift into another state which seems to be dominated by the right brain. Or they will become involved in describing an event in Vietnam and enter much the same state. In this state the language of the patient changes and his ideas change. He relies on standard swear words to convey meaning. Adjectives drop our and are replaced by expletives and forceful inflections which convey the meaning. Ideas become more visual and pictorial. Usually the patient also displays the somatic symptoms of stress. The most common word that is used is "fucking" which can be inserted in any part of a sentence or even between syllables of a word. There is deep meaning behind the choice of this word, it seems to me. It refers to procreation, which is sorely needed in a world filled with death. When the veterans are in this state they remind me of left stroke patients who are unable to converse but can swear and sing words. The result of military training is not only the shortening of the reaction time but a profound change in the identity of the individual soldier. When entering the service the person is stripped of his uniqueness in many ways: he is dressed the same as all the others, his hair is cut the same way, he does the same things as everyone else and does it at the same time in the same group. He is told what to do and is discouraged from thinking on his own. He is thought of as a member of the "outfit" or the service. He is a part of a whole and is no longer a whole himself. People outside of the group are counted as unimportant. The enemy is evil and seen as the cause of all bad things. The buddy is all good and needs to be preserved at any cost. The soldier is prepared to die for his buddy and knows that the buddy will die for him if necessary. In the war this experience was imprinted on the individual during the years of 18, 19, and 20 when the personality is first learning about being in the world as an adult. It seems to the soldier that what he is experiencing is the norm and a pattern to be continued throughout life. Consequently the close relationships formed in war have some very unique qualities. They tend to be without ambivalence since the enemy was seen as all bad and the buddy was idealized as all good. There is fusion in this relationship. Because of the individual identity having been replaced by a group identity the buddies feel that they are almost a part of each other. The support from such relationships is one of the few friendly and helpful elements in an otherwise hostile environment. Understandably the buddy is idealized and overvalued, especially in retrospect. The serviceman returns to this country with the notion that close relationships are all of this character. Unfortunately such relationships are not found outside of life and death situations. The patient struggles to recapture the support he felt with his buddy but is doomed to disappointment. Here close relationships require sensitivity to feelings and of course feelings are kept carefully away from the patient's consciousness or if experienced they are seen as threatening requiring immediate defenses such as numbing or anger. This process can interfere with the therapeutic relationship. The therapist needs to be constantly aware of the patient's disability in the area of feelings. Anger needs to be reinterpreted as the threat of underlying feelings. This whole dynamic changes when the veteran has experienced the death of a close buddy. Then the veteran anticipates loss with every relationship and becomes more depressed and isolated. As the patient becomes more knowledgeable about himself he becomes aware of changes happening within him. Patients will report a change in their flashback phenomena. First they have experience that place then in Vietnam without any awareness of the current surroundings. Gradually they notice that even while experiencing scenes from Vietnam they are also aware of their current reality. This dual reality is frightening and the patient is grateful for any explanation that can be provided him. I interpret this phenomenon as an example of the individual being aware of both the right and left-brain activity. Another painful change is the increasing awareness of the losses that were sustained in war. These can be either obvious or subtle. Not only friends are lost but also parts of the individual are list, e.g. body parts, sets of values, confidence in the self, etc. Even loved objects require mourning. Currently I am trying help a veteran with the loss of his airplane. He still bursts into tears when he unexpectedly sees such a plane flying. Mourning is normal and natural but its symptoms closely resemble many of the symptoms of PTSD.

The symptom of survival guilt has been a curious one to me. It never seemed to be explained and the patients cannot give an explanation for it. When the patient is able to describe his experience fairly completely I found that it always had the quality of being chaotic, meaningless, and unexplainable. The human mind abhors meaninglessness and attempts to explain everything. The explanation of survival guilt is found in this characteristic of people. When faced with a situation of chaos and lack of meaning by blaming himself for what was wrong and this supplies meaning where there was none. The same phenomenon is seen in the two-year-old child who tries to explain what is happening to him but does not have the knowledge of experience to interpret complicated situations.

Perhaps the most valuable tool in dealing with these patients is the skill of recognizing when the patient is having a stress reaction. This is rather easily accomplished by carefully observing the physical signs of the fight-flight reflex. Respiration increases, heart rate increases, blood pressure increases. The patient breaks into a sweat, often literally dripping. His eyes become dark, the "black look." This is the result of the pupils dilating. Often gastrointestinal sounds can be heard. Frequently the patient trembles. His state of consciousness changes to right brain dominance with its typical thought style, vocabulary, etc.

The appearance of these phenomena can be used in therapy to identify the precipitating thought or event, which has just occurred in the therapeutic hour. So far I have been talking about symptoms that are the result of the trauma that occurred in war. There is another source of trauma for these veterans and that is the unusual events, which took place in this country when it reneged on the warrior contract, a traditional and clear contract. Young men assume the role of warrior by placing themselves in the position of giving their lives for their country if necessary. In turn the country promises to honor them and welcome them into an important status in the society. As you know many of the veterans describe being exposed to degrading acts from people when they returned home. This seemed to confirm their growing awareness that they had been pawns in a chaotic political process. Their response to this was to feel exploited and betrayed. This feeling appears frequently in therapy and in their everyday lives. Any authority is suspect of taking advantage of them. The therapist cannot expect to be helpful to them if he or she allow himself or herself to be aligned with authorities that are seen as corrupt. Finally, as in all therapy, these patients are experiencing much suffering. When anyone is suffering talk is not primarily helpful. The person needs to be accepted and accompanied in his grief and pain. The therapist needs to be there while the patient shares his hurt with an accepting and supportive figure.

Dr. E.S.

Hearing

I am Dean Kurtz, Hearing Officer. Mr. Connelly is present and is represented by Tom Hanson of the VFW.

Mr. Connelly would you remain seated please, but raise your right hand?

Do you swear or affirm that the testimony you are about to give is the truth:

I do.

Thank you, sir. The issue that we have before us today is service connection for post-traumatic stress disorder. If that is correct, Mr. Hanson, you may proceed.

Thank you, we believe that the veteran is, in fact, entitled to service connection for post traumatic stress disorder. We understand that he had previously submitted two claims for service connection for ptsd and that those two decisions were unfavorable and he did not appeal. He did not appeal because he believed, at the time, the evidence of record may not have been sufficient to substantiate his claim. We do, however, believe that the statement by Dr. Edwin Smelker from The Post Traumatic Stress Recovery Unit does, in fact, or should, in fact, constitute new and material evidence and does form a new factual basis upon which service connection can be granted. It is our belief that this evidence does meet the criteria of Title 38 U.S.C. 1156 or whatever the citation is relative to a well grounded claim. And we believe that on the basis that prior to this, we don't believe that any of the evidence that had been submitted actually rendered a positive diagnosis of ptsd and we believe that the statement by Dr. Smelker does, in fact, diagnose ptsd with major depressive episodes and it is our belief that statement from Dr. Smelker does constitute a new factual basis. More so, we believe that service connection is in order based on that statement more so than the rating examination that was given to Mr. Connelly when he saw Dr. Whitaker and Dr. Whitaker apparently felt that the more appropriate diagnosis was a dysthymic disorder or generalized anxiety reaction. We believe that Dr. Smelker is in a far better position to render a more accurate diagnosis being the treating physician that Dr. Whitaker who merely saw the veteran for a 20 minute period. As a matter of fact, Mr. Connelly has informed me that he had been treated by Dr. Smelker for two years before Dr. Smelker rendered the diagnosis simply because of the fact that he was unsure himself and if, in fact, his treating physican was unsure, certainly we understand where Dr. Whitaker would be unsure of a diagnosis, but as a result of that, it is our belief that Dr. Smelker's diagnosis is more appropriate because of the fact that he has continued to treat Mr. Connelly and is more aware of the symptomatology and the stressors that, in fact, he bases his diagnosis on. And as a result of those, those actions, we also believe that there may, in fact, be some question as to the stressors. I notice, in the Statement of Case that was issued in the Reasons for Decision section, the Rating Board members chose to believe, quote-unquote, Dr. Whitaker's statement over that of Dr. Smelker on the basis that they did not believe that the evidence of record supported the diagnosis of ptsd. It appears one of the main reasons was that they did not, in fact, believe that Mr. Connelly had described or sufficiently described, the stressors or that he had experienced an event that was outside the range of the usual human experience and Mr. Connelly has informed me, this morning, that he has, in fact prepared a statement that he would like to submit today that more thoroughly describes his stressors and he would like to submit evidence this time and he also has some other evidence that he would like to submit and maybe you can describe to Mr. Kurtz, at this time, Tim what it is you have as additional evidence that you wish to submit.

I have a statement of some experiences I went through and I have two Unit Citations that, for the time I was there, indicating that we were short personnel and had numerous mass casualty situations. And I don't know if you are interested in my Social Security report or not, but that indicates some of my social employabilites, stuff like that.

Mr Hanson: So this is virtually what we will be submitting is, in fact, Mr. Connelly's personal statement, copies of two Unit citations and a summary of the examination that he received from the Social Security Administration, in fact, describes some social and industrial situations. Anything else that you want to submit at this time, Tim?

Mr. Connelly: Do you people ever read these? I have some literature on, on medical professionals and ptsd and stuff like that. I don't know if that would be of interest to the board.

Mr. Kurtz: It may very well be, yes. I'd be very happy to see that.

Mr. Connelly: Okay, I'll enter that.

Mr. Kurtz: The records that you referred to from the Social Security, I think you referred to them, Tom, and an examination?

Mr. Hanson: Yes

Mr. Kurtz: Did you undergo a separate examination by Social Security or did they base their findings on existing records.

Mr. Connelly: They based their finds on existing records. I went before an Administrative Law judge.

Mr. Hanson: The questions that I have, I guess, are rather general and may, in fact, include some of the information in your statement. The first question that I'd like to ask is, what, in fact, your military occupational skill was when you were in Vietnam?

Mr. Connelly: 91-20 which was a clinical specialist, like a civilian practical nurse.

Mr. Hanson: And you worked where?

I worked in the Intensive Care Unit, the Neuro Unit, the Emergency Room, Recovery Room and I worked with Vietnamese patients for awhile and the last few months, at a dispensary.

Mr. Hanson: This was located where?

Mr. Connelly: In Long Binh

Mr. Hanson: Okay and you were constantly involved with treating casualties or what this periodically or sporadically or…

Mr. Connelly: Constantly. It was, most of the other hospitals were shutting down around the country and we were getting most of the casualties from that area, so it was on the go all the time.

Mr. Hanson: When did you serve in Vietnam?

Mr. Connelly: !970-1971

Mr. Hanson: And as hospital personnel working in, was this an EVAC hospital or general hospital or…

Mr. Connelly: It was 24th EVAC hospital.

Mr. Hanson: Okay and your, do you believe that in that statement you have submitted your stressors are explained very thoroughly or would you like to review those or put those on the record today?

Mr. Connelly: I have a short statement here I could read.

The intensive care unit, recovery room, emergency room, and neuro unit are areas that I worked on during my first few months in Vietnam. The typical patients would be like a double amputee, no legs, the bones and muscles and everything showing like a piece of meat in a butcher shop. I would assist in many ways, cutting off uniforms, checking wounds, putting in IVs or hold a patient who was struggling while the doctor would put a breathing tube in his throat. The sights, smells and sounds of the wounded and dying are hard to describe. The raspy, rattling breathing, the gurgling fluids and at times, my uniform and body were covered with blood. We had a lot of belly wounds in the ICU and the smell was awful, kind of like being at a rendering plant. Also we had patients with amputations and burn cases and other traumatic wounds. The first patient to die on me was a POW. We threw his body in a green bag like a, you know, like a bale of straw and took him to the morgue which was a small building at the other end of the hospital. It was a room that looked like a miniature barracks for a concentration camp inmates. They had wooded planks stacked like bunks in which the body was placed. The problem was that, being my first body bagging, I forgot that I was supposed to remove some tubes and stuff and tag the body. The wardmaster made me go back to make things right. In the meantime, other body bags had been placed in the morgue and the guy wasn't where we put him in the first place so I had to look through a few bags before I found the right one. I remember the open mouths and blank stares of the dead as I searched for the POW. Another incident by the morgue involved a mass casualty situation. I was sent to the recovery room to help with the overflow. I took a short break and went outside where about a dozen body bags were stacked and a couple of guys were going through them looking for personal effects and identification. On the ICU we treated burn patients. I recall two guys who were burned over 90 percent of their bodies. They were swollen like balloons. We couldn't identify their features or even their race. The smell was terrible and when dressings had to be changed, the screams of pain were piercing to the ear. You felt like you were hurting them when you were trying to help them when you were trying to help them. They eventually died. Or the guy with the chest wound who went into cardiac arrest and I'm the only person around for a few minutes and I'm going through the CPR routine until the rest of the team gets there and the fibrillator doesn't work and the doctor cuts his chest open to massage the heart and I'm fumbling with the AMBU bag to help the guy breathe, but the guy dies and he's just laying there split open, staring at me, so one of the other guys sews up his chest and we put him in a bag and take him down to the morgue. What I hated was telling someone that things were okay when you knew they weren't going to make it. How do you tell a guy everything is going to be all right as you're holding his artery in your hand and the blood's gushing all over the place, or the guy with the hole in his chest that you can put both arms through or you're scooping blood clots out of a guy's back which has been ripped off or guys whose whole insides have been blown away and you're trying to keep from tossing your cookies. the guy who lost both legs and an arm and rolls out of bed, tries to kill himself by raising the bed with one good arm and dropping it on his throat, but he missed and you pick up this quivering piece of meat which is yelling to die. I also worked for a few months strictly with Vietnamese patients, children to old adults, many shrapnel and burn wounds, along with being exposed to polio, TB, hepatitis, plague, smallpox and leprosy. The burned and maimed children were the hardest to deal with, but I started to appreciate the Vietnamese and wanted to learn more about their culture. The mamma sans would stay with their kids and help us out by doing various chores like emptying the trash and stuff like that to be helpful. I was displeased with the racism that was evident among others I worked with at during that time frame. The burn patients would be in a lot of pain. Most would just lay there and wait to die. Sometimes a rocket or something would be aimed at the ammo dump and the doors would blow open and stuff would fall off the walls. We has a routine by which we would put the patients that were able on the floor under the beds and those bedridden, we would cover with mattresses. Of course, we had no weapons to defend ourselves, but I did carry a .38 snub nose in my pocket, taken from a wounded pilot, as protection against the unknown, not only the VC, but the enemy within, the drug users who would scare the hell out of me because you couldn't trust them. I got into fights with them, and at one point, held the barrel of my pistol to this fellow's temple saying I would blow his head off if he didn't get his stuff together because we were supposed to be on alert. Sappers did hit the front gate a couple if times, one time while I was on guard duty, but I was far enough away that I just watched the action of the gunships. Working on the neuro ward was difficult because you have patients that had their brains scrambled or blown away. You had to do everything for them. I really had a very difficult time working with these patients and walked off the ward one day because it was just too much to handle. So I would be sent back to the ICU to work with guys like the one with an infected chest wound, the pus oozing out the sides of the bandages and the nauseating smell of rotten flesh. That also was getting to me after six months, or was it seven, I forget. The constant routine, the last few months I got to work on those who had been hit by shrapnel or other wounds. I would cut away the dead tissue and clean the wounds and then three days later, suture the wounds with steel suture. But the fact was that by that time, people had become wounds and I was, as hard as I could to, I worked hard as I could to avoid situations in which someone was dying, then one day, it was all over, but I felt guilty about leaving. During the whole year I had not taken any time off for such things as R&R or whatever and now it was time to go and yet, I don't feel I had accomplished much during my tour of duty. That would be my statement.

Mr. Hanson: Okay, Now, how long have you been treated over at the PTSR unit with Dr. Smelker?

Mr. Connelly: About five years.

Mr. Hanson: And you've been going there on a regular basis?

Mr. Connelly: Weekly and bi-weekly for individual therapy and monthly medication refills and I also do some volunteering over there.

Mr: Hanson: Okay, and what medication has he got you prescribed now?

Mr. Connelly: 60mg of Prozac, 100mg of Trazodone, 4 mg of Valium and I take 50 to 100mg of Benadryl for sleep at night.

Mr. Hanson: Okay and have you continued to partake in any of the group therapies that he has over there?

Mr. Connelly: I have trouble with the groups, so I've stayed, I've stayed in the, mostly with individual therapy.

Mr. Hanson: Okay, and you shy away from the group therapy because of the experiences that they describe or what's your reasons for that?

Mr. Connelly: There just seems to be too many people in the group. I just, when I first went through the program, there was six people in a group for several weeks and that was, that was okay, but after you get out of the program, they have larger groups with ten or 15 people in them. I didn't feel like it was therapeutic enough, I guess. You only get about five minutes to talk. I, I didn't like going.

Mr. Hanson: Okay, Now, your situation at the Minnesota Veterans Home, do you have a private room over there or do you share a room...

Mr. Connelly: Actually, I just got a private room last, last week on the recommendation of the PTSD program.

Mr. Hanson: Okay and that was because of your...

Mr. Connelly: Sleeping problems and so forth.

Mr. Hanson: Okay and do you feel better when you're isolated or...

Mr. Connelly: I feel safer.

Mr. Hanson: Okay and do you have any friends at the Veterans Home?

Mr. Connelly: Not real friends, superficial type, you know, it's hi, how's things going, or I can sit with somebody at dinner or whatever, but no real close friends. I've never been on a social event since I've been there and that's been three years.

Mr. Hanson: Okay, you, when you go to the mess hall or anything like that, do you, you know, can you describe maybe some of the activities that, or mind things that you go through relative to where you seat yourself and that type of thing?

Mr. Connelly: Usually it's, I wait until most of the crowd has gone through, so I go later, about 5:00 when there's only a couple of people in line or you can get through the line right away. And then I usually sit towards the back of the dining hall or in a position where I'm exposed to what's going on or what's coming in.

Mr. Hanson: Do you own an automobile so that you can leave the grounds or anything like that?

Mr. Connelly: No automobile, I've never, never had a car.

Mr. Hanson: Okay. What do you do for hobbies or activities or anything like that? Do you have any of those types of things that you entertain yourself with?

Mr. Connelly: Reading and TV is probably about the only thing I, I have been taking a course or two at a technical college to try to see if I can get back into things, but that's been very difficult because I, I'm afraid to ride the bus. I get really anxious on the bus, but I, the concentration level comes and goes, but I've made it through a couple of classes.

Mr. Hanson: Okay How many hours of sleep do you figure you get in a night?

Mr. Connelly: Four on a good night, but now they've got ne on some sleeping medication and that seems to help, but it takes me an hour, sometimes two hours, to get to sleep and I'll wake up every hour on the hour type of thing.

Mr. Hanson: Okay and you experience nightmares on a regular basis or...

Mr. Connelly: It's sporatic. I had one, in fact, I had one two weeks ago and I don't know why. I haven't had one for a few months, but I jumped out of my bed screaming and yelling, running out towards the door and I, that's when I still had a roommate and I think I scared the heck out of him, but...

Mr. Hanson: Does that, these nightmares you experience, are those the same theme or the same nightmare, or do those change or...

Mr. Connelly: There's a couple, there's one I go through all the bodies, the faces of all the bodies. For something, I don't know, sometimes something triggers it off, a guy dies at the home or something and unconsciously that will trigger off some things or, a guy committed suicide I think, a couple of weeks ago and maybe that triggered that off. But you know, and there's another one where I fear of being overrun, you know, that never happened or anything, but I still have this fear that I'm going to be overrun or whatever, you know, like I'm on guard duty some place and that's been a periodic dream, but it never actually happened, but I mean, it's just that feeling that, for that dream.

Mr. Hanson: Okay, well I guess you know the only the only other things that I may want to address in your issue is that your stressors were involved with treating these casualties and the dead and that type of thing more so than seeing a guy getting blown up or the actual experience of, combat per se. Is that virtually what I, what you're trying to say here, Tim, or...

Mr. Connelly: Well, according to the DSM3R, the, you know the essential feature of this post traumatic stress is development of a characteristic symptom following a psychologically distressing event that is outside the range of usual human experience, outside the range of such common experiences of simple bereavement, chronic illness, business losses and marital conflict and the problems combat vets experience may begin during or after combat trauma or may be delayed for many years. The stressors may be military conflict, prolonged exposure to death and casualties as experienced by medics, nurses, physicians or POWs. So that's the point I'm working on, seeing another person who have been seriously injured or killed as a result of an accident or physical violence. I think I've seen that.

Mr. Hanson: Okay, I have nothing further, at this time, Mr. Kurtz. Thank you.

Mr. Kurtz: Thank you. Mr. Connelly is there anything else you would like to say before we close the hearing?

Mr. Connelly: I just think that, in the position I'm in now, maybe a small amount of service connection, 30 percent say would be enough to enable me to get back into functioning enough to get out of the Vets Home and might make me eligible for more educational benefits to get my life going instead of marking time like I am, seem to be doing. I think it would be beneficial, I mean, the condition, as I've heard from other people, you know, can get, can improve and the disability can go down and so forth, so, but at the immediate time, I think any help that I can get would be beneficial for me to keep moving on instead of just ending up in the Vets Home, which I don't want to do. that's it.

Mr. Kurtz: We will terminate the hearing then…

Like Father...Like Son

His father wondered if there was anything he could do to help his son. It was a big shock when the boy entered the Army. The family didn't expect him to enlist. When the boy wrote home from basic training all he was told to do was kill, kill, kill, kill... When he came home from the war he seemed in pretty good shape but stayed at home and drank. His father had done the same thing after World War II. The father minimized his four years in the South Pacific with the Marines and tried more or less to forget about it. His father didn't have any nightmares but certain dates were bad...like Christmas. When his father was a kid on the farm he never thought of war and was totally unprepared. The father and son used to get together but the son has never been back home since my mothers death some years ago.

Vulnerable

He attended a session about the family with some other men. He sat quietly and listened attentively and didn't miss one word. He predictably interjected some emotionally impactful statement which was always extremely accurate and indicative of his insight and ability to pull things together and point it out in such a way that the other men understood. He talked about being rocketed once in awhile and having no bunker to which to escape and therefore had to remain with the sick and wounded while the enemy fire continued. He put patients under the bed and those that were no able to move were covered with mattresses. He was not issued a weapon so he was even more vulnerable and unable to defend himself.

To Whom It May Concern

He came to us a caring, sensitive, idealistic, innocent and supremely unprepared for providing the enormously stressful type of patient care. He tried his best and never refused to work or function at what he was capable of doing, but he simply was not cut ot to be a medic. There was no lack of intellect nor desire...the difficulty was of a too great a sensitivity to the pain and suffering of patients. To demand that he function in the capacity of a medic was inappropriate, there were an infinite number of other places that would have been grateful for his abilities. He became a victim of a system that could not tolerate or condone individuality. He has considered himself a failure since that sorrowful time those many years ago, but the saddest part of it is that it was needless, as he was an intelligent, sensitive human being with many wonderful and redeeming qualities. The untold anguish borne by him for all these years seems to be a common denominator of so many of those who served in his capacity.

Capt. P. Kettlewell USA

Hate

The picture in the newspaper showed some troops dragging a wounded enemy soldier out of a ditch. As the man begged for his life, he was shot. Other troops expressed joy in the man's demise. As a soldier, he had learned that it didn't take much effort to hate. Some humans even made it much easier to hate because their actions were so evil. However, to hurt someone who was already wounded seemed very cruel. Medics could be cruel, too. He watched as the head nurse abused and maltreated a prisoner of war who was wounded and scared. What could he do? It was war and the man was the enemy. The patient couldn't fight back but deserved to be treated like a human being. It was hard for him to hate someone who was all shot to hell and afraid. He felt people were all the same and shared the same needs of survival on the planet. He often wondered if he had been born in a far off land if he would have become the enemy.

How susceptible we had been to rhetoric and ritual. We had yearned for something to believe in, like justice. We had been made vulnerable and sent off to war, passed a sense of obligation by our elders to believe in the glory of war. Inspired Catholic boys and girls rallied to the call of JFK to fight communists everywhere, to satisfy not only our parents, teachers and priests...but God, Pope and President. War seemed beyond all doubt a good thing and a form of virtue. However, our belief in all authority became disillusion along with a sense of loss which made us feel like orphans cut off from a sustaining world of church, state and parents. All sources of moral truth and authority dissolved exposing us to human culpability and brutality and to wonder.

A Rebel...With No Cause

People often asked him what he was going to do with his life. he would tell them he gave half of his life to the nation and the rest now belonged to him. He wanted to be a rebel and didn't want to conform anymore. He could go to war but when it was all over he had to resume a normal life and work and live as if there had never been any horror. Of course, it never worked that way. He was self-conscious and traumatized by harsh judgment. He feared that everything he touched would become contaminated. It was hard for him to imagine anything but negative responses so he tried very little, becoming distracted for days, months, years. A sense of mastery eluded him and he became overwhelmed by a sense of being incompetent. Invisible like a ghost. No threat, just not quite all here or there.

Intrusive Thought

He had this recurring dream of being in a room, surrounded by bodies and parts of bodies laid side by side. The air smelled of diesel oil. His job was to get the names, ages and hometowns of the dying victims. He never got by the first victim before He got sick and someone told him to go home. He begged to stay and that's when he would awake horrified. He never knew if he was horrified by the room full of death or his inability to get the job done. Inside all the details of death had accumulated but he missed that jolt of adrenaline, and the wholesome insanity and unhealthy pace. Part of him still remained a medic in a crowded, noisy, windowless room.

Therapy BS

Hell was group therapy. The talk was mostly bullshit. There were a lot of war stories. How true they were was anyone's guess. He sat silent in the corner. They were in group for their war crimes by appointment of the devil. "Tell the doctors what you are feeling." "What is the problem?" "Why are you angry.? " He was just fed up with being a veteran. He should have taken a vow of silence but then they would think he was withdrawing and give him more pills. Group therapy was driving him nuts. Was he cursed to spend the rest of my days sitting in a circle? Didn't they understand that he had gone to war and hurt. So don't tell him how to act or what to do. He followed the one true VA way and where did it get him....group therapy.

He was a rebel in therapy. The VA way was not the only way to a better life. It only made him bitter. Therapy was Mickey Mouse crap. He didn't want to make any damn wallet. He had no money to put in it. He didn't want to paint a picture of the Last Supper by the numbers, since Jesus didn't give a damn about him, either. Let him create what he wanted, not what the system wanted. Let him dream.

The Home

It was Hell's House. The Vet's Home was a place for old, sick, and homeless veterans. The buildings were from another century, worn like the men and women they housed. How did he get into this mess? He just wanted to be a normal person and live a happy life. What would happen to him? Would he ever leave the Home on his own power and not on a morgue cart? It was like being in film noir. His room was dark and hot and colorless. The stench of urine rose from the carpet as a mouse whizzed along a worn baseboard. He would sit by the window eating and watching as men shuffled back and forth between the buildings. The buildings were condemned much like the residents. Men worried about what would become of them. The State liked to keep them worried, that way they wouldn't be ungrateful for all the care and attention it provided. The WWII veterans hated the younger veterans. The younger vets hadn't been in real wars and whined too much. They should be out working. They should be anywhere but near them. The Greatest Generation had always been a pain in his ass.

Daily Grind

He wanted to runaway but where would he go. He would just keep
running into himself and that was getting old. He wanted to run but He
was out of shape. There was to much weight on his shoulders, too
much pain in his soul. He would sit by the river, rain or shine, warm or
cold and watched the boats go by with the tan babes on deck. Were
they real? Did they feel sad and lonely? He sat by the river as life
passed him by. They found a headless body in the river one day and a
man tried to cut off a woman's legs in the picnic area. A war zone on
the Mississippi. Some days it felt like a prison, other days a funny
farm. Guys lined up an hour ahead of time for chow, just to be first.
Veterans loved to complain about anything. It reminded then of their
military days. They bitched about the food which was heavy on meat,
gravy and grease. It was bland but so filling. The finest chefs could
prepare meals and the veterans would find something wrong. It was
not uncommon for someone to toss their plate against the wall and
yell..."SHIT".

A dark mood overwhelmed him and he would turn to his favorite remedy, eating junk food. He would get an urge for Spam and Cheese Whiz on Wonder Bread. Cheeseburger Hamburger Helper and ice cream sandwiches. His weight was near 400 pounds. His only exercise was going to the store for more food. Clothes were hard to find. His pants were big and baggy and His shirts were small tents. He had grown a beard to hide behind and enhance his ugly image. He sweated and smelled like meat. His own personalized hell. No one would hire a big, fat, ugly guy. No one could love a big, fat, ugly guy. Eating one's self to death was so time consuming

He got 52 dollars a month from welfare but wanted more. The cure was to get a job. All would be well if he had a job. He would feel good if he had a job. He would be part of the human race with a job. He wanted a job. But not another blow job, not another hand job, not another snow job. His ideal job would be to eliminate all the bullshit. He would never be out of work.

Compensation

The social worker said he didn't deserve any disability money. "It's for those that really got hurt." He was suppose to pull himself up by the bootstraps and forget it. But he didn't have any boots and he didn't want to forget. If he got some compensation, maybe he could start living like a real person in a house and a quiet neighborhood and not feel that he was going to be attacked at any moment. The compensation path wasn't easy. It was a trip equal to climbing Mount Everest or traveling into the deepest jungles of the Amazon. Strange creatures and hazards at every turn. The veteran traveled at their own risk, unless they were lucky enough to get a guide. Many were swallowed by the unknown, never to be heard from again.

The Exam

The exam doctor looked like the poster child for death. "What's bothering you?" "Did you have problems before you went to war?" "Can you sleep at night." "How long have you had this drinking problem?" "Have you sought treatment?" Are you afraid of different people?" "Do you hear voices?" The doctor had his list of symptoms. It was like a high school quiz. Match the question to the right answer but what was the right answer. It better fit the doctor's guidelines or you lost. The system would get you if you didn't watch out. The world didn't owe veterans a living, he thought , but somebody owed them something for being the whores of war.

Too Young To Be An Old Soldier

He was too young to be an old soldier. In fact, he was to young to have
been a soldier in the first place. It seemed like he would be in the Old
Soldiers Home for the rest of his life. He felt like a deflated tire and it
was hard to hold back the tears. His life was changing and he couldn't
seem to do anything about it. He was catching old age from the old
soldiers. His weight was skyrocketing. His cholesterol had turned bad.
His blood had become sugar. His butt bled. Who gave a damn? The
Home was more concerned about getting his money than it did about
his care and treatment. Old soldiers didn't die...they rotted away in the
depths of places like the Veterans Home.

The Game

He was being followed at the VA Medical Center and remained totally disabled by his problems and was unable to work at any gainful employment. His problem continued to bother him with dreams and nightmares. He lived in fear which made it difficult for him to leave his room or ride the bus. He felt on guard all the time and had chronic sleep problems. He was unable to be close to others and led a very isolated lifestyle. It sounded like he was really bad news but those were the words that had to be used. Just so he didn't start believing it himself and fall into the helpless trap like so many other guys had done. It was like their lives had stopped and they had become professional patients.

The Memory of War

It was sometimes subtle, like a mist creeping low across the water, creeping into every corner of his life. It reminded him of the child's terror dream but yet from a dream one could not awake. Seeing nothing else but that which passes through a filter dimming the visions of the world. It was a sense of falling into a bottomless pit, looking for an end but seeing none. His sense of life before was vague, leaving a sensation of pain with no beginning or end. He would cry out for help, but was not heard. There was a lot of sadness, grief raged unresolved within. War pursued and haunted an obsession throughout. The war was over except in dreams and thoughts. He imagined he would never forget. The bomb of memory exploded into a red hot flame and nothing was able to put out the fire.

Dead Vet

His friend Joe was buried on a Friday and it was probably safe to say only a few people would miss him. Joe died at the age of 55 in the hospital at which he had first sought some answers more than 20 years ago. Those few who did know him talked about his smile, his easy wit and his kindness for all. Joe had walked away from friends and family 25 years ago. An uncle once tried a number of times to contact him but it never came about. The uncle felt Joe was now "free" and didn't have to be anything to anybody. Joe had been a soldier, a college graduate, a writer, a laborer, and a drunk...his longest role. He had held jobs but not for long. He wrote about war, poverty and alcohol but somewhere along the line his life snapped and went to hopelessness, failure, and self destruction. That somewhere was the war. It was puzzling to see Joe without a job because he was smart, looked strong and had the ability to connect to people.

He wanted to help Joe but he couldn't even help himself let alone someone else.

Confession

Bless him father for he had sinned. He had tried to follow the rules and believe in God, but it had become a struggle. A fight between the spiritual self and the religious self. He came home from a war with ideas in conflict. Reality didn't match up with the values he had been taught. He felt used and thrown away. All he had sensed over the years was apathy. He could no longer believe in the goodness of God. His soul had left and he want it back.

Priority Care

A call came at day's end. His doctor's appointment had been canceled.
Nothing new. "No, you don't understand, the doctor has retired,
sorry." That's the government... and have a nice day too. There was
no honor. Somebody had to do something. Sadness and anger
consumed him. He feared his health would suffer. The system had
failed him once again. His healthcare had been put in jeopardy once
again. He felt like a beggar. Screwed once again. No one cared. Wave
the flag, rattle the saber, buy the message, serve your country and end
up in line, waiting all the time, cursing the day he bought the bullshit.

The Daily War

For most people, wars are relegated to history. For other people, war becomes part of their daily lives. War is in their dreams, affects their families, their jobs and the way they relate to the world. Forever stranded in that place and time, spirit as well as body wounded and defiled. After returning from war, they are proud not because they are happy to have gone to war -- the human part of man should be ashamed he went to war -- that part of him which feels pride is the vain part of man, the empty part of man. The human part has the shame. Who better represents the preciousness of life, the need for peace and the human cost of making war.

He was opposed to permitting homosapiens in the military. To do so will greatly harm the morale and combat capability of our proud and tough fighting forces. The military will be a haven for homosapiens committed to practicing their ungodly lifestyle rather than defending our nation. Homosapiens should not be in the military in any capacity and those already in should be kicked out.

Mr. Excitement

There was a special on TV about the Great Depression. He watched because He thought it was about his life. He went to talk therapy but his therapist was a mime. He didn't have any friends so he got the infrequent callers rate. He had call not waiting on his phone. He wanted to be a priest. They told him he was too celibate. He joined the army to be a killer. They made him a medic. He should have gone to Canada. He couldn't speak Canadian. He was going to write a book. "He Saw The Whores Of War And Their Prices Were Reasonable." He thought he got sprayed by chemical warfare. Every spring, he found himself chasing Chem Lawn Trucks.

Does Anyone Know What Time It Is?

Mr. Kline was a social worker at the VA hospital. He never really
wanted to be working at the VA, but there he was from nine to five
each day. His job was to get a person on the road to employment. Even
if you went to Harvard Law School, he always told people to get a job
at Wal-Mart and live the American lower class dream. It was his
mantra. He was a snob who hated his job. In group therapy, he told us
how to use our spare time. A hobby would be good. He said he
collected clocks from all around the world. I raised my hand..."Mr
Kline, I bet time really flies around your house..." Everyone laughed,
except Mr. Kline. A man's hobby is not a laughing matter. "Perhaps
you have too much time on your hands," I added. We all laughed while
Mr. Kline looked at his watch and reminded me my time was running
out.

War Persists

The history of the world is the history of war. Each war different. Stories about war share something in common. How men fight. Where men fight. How men and women die. War consists of actions that no one would otherwise perform. War persists in the mind throughout a lifetime. Questions are asked. What happened? Who was I? Who did I become? A generation that has lived through a war is different. Within a war generation those who fought stand apart from those who did not. There's a need to record, to find meaning, to find themselves.

Farewell

It was raining on the trip to the airport. They used his uncle's car. It had more room than their old wreck. His father, mother, brother and sister had all come along to bid him farewell. He had to catch an early morning flight. Except for the chatter coming from the radio everyone sat in silence. His dad smoked a Salem, while his mom cradled his little sister in her arms. His brother sat next to him half asleep. In his army uniform, he gazed out the window at the passing brown grass, bare farm fields, and occasional road kill. He wasn't thinking about going to war, but how he was going to say good-by. It wouldn't be an emotional affair. A hug for mom, a handshake for dad and a wave to brother and sister and then down the ramp glad to be on his way.

Ying and Yang

The plane comes through the clouds as smoke rises from the hill sides below. His heart was thumping, his stomach turning, his mind racing. He was landing in hell but it looked like paradise. He felt the intense heat as he rushed to the armor-plated bus. It surely was hell how convenient, he wouldn't have far to go when he died. The bus sped down the road passing sandbagged bunkers with machine guns on the white sand mounds. The smell of burning feces and the sounds of war in the distance. A gentle breeze blew across the hot white beach as blue waves lapped against the shore. In the officers club, a young girl served chilled drinks to men in white suits and women in formal dress as music played in the background and the war raged. Back home his mother wondered about her first born.

The Dead

Small white stones laid out in orderly rows atop a barren windblown
hill the graves of civilians killed by an air strike the dead were buried
soon after death no headstones or written information about them. It's
tradition. They were friends They fought against a common enemy
Now the friends are all dead a lone man wipes a tear trembling, he
pauses which one of the graves is his father's If he had the means he
would fight against the killers.

Breathe

Stop, listen. Breathe you bastard! Don't die on me! Breathe. Stop, Listen. He was afraid. His heart was pounding, out of control. "Are you awake dear? She stroked his back and whispered in his ear, "It's only a dream, my darling." They lie still and breathe in unison. Her warm body, soft and safe. As they cuddle, his fear vanishes and he breathes a sigh of relief.

War

What is the true cost of war? A decade after the elder Bush's war thousands of former soldiers struggle for benefits and medical care for sickness caused by toxins. What is the true cost of war? More than a quarter of a century since troops left Southeast Asia we still witness the effects on those former soldiers of homelessness, substance abuse, mental illness, and isolation. They feel forgotten by their country. What is the true cost of war? Nearly a lifetime has passed since WWII and still former soldiers suffer from illness and depression. What is the true cost of war? The true cost of war can't be measured, and now we must come to terms with another war and the problems it will cause for a new generation touched by war. We can only hope and wait and try to inform about the true effects of war. Listen to my voice as one who was put in harm's way for this country. War causes wounds and suffering that last beyond the battlefield.

Duty

He didn't know their names. They weren't people. They were gunshot wound lower back, multiple frag wound, traumatic amputation or KIA. He beat on their chests, breathed his air into their lungs and held their bleeding arteries in his naked hands. He watched them suffer. He watched them die. He put them in bags. He took them to a shed. They had names but that was no concern of his. He had a job to do. He couldn't let that stuff get to him or he would no longer be of any use.

Shit Detail

The first few days at war were spent in a replacement company. They weren't getting any travel orders so they were put on work details. A private came along and told a few of them to get into a truck. The private took them to a latrine. The private handed each of them a pair of gloves and told them to start carrying cans full of feces so he could burn the contents. They looked at each other and then began pulling the pots which looked and smelled like something out of hell. The private then poured gasoline into the pots and set them on fire. A sacrifice to the gods of war? The private had been burning shit for eight months and only had four months left on the latrine detail. "What the hell," he said, " somebody has to burn crap for freedom and democracy."

Guard Duty

He hated the damn heat. What was out there beyond the wire? Some evil little man or woman plotting his demise. By day it looked so green and peaceful but at night that all vanished into a black wall. He sat alone not knowing what he would do if something happened. Every little noise made him turn. He could hear the war in the distance. Would it come closer tonight? He watched the flares float along the night sky. AN EXPLOSION! He jumped. It was off to the right. He heard small arms fire. Another flare. He didn't know what the hell was going on. A helicopter gunship fired into the blackness. The tracer rounds danced in the air, so surreal. He sat and watched to fascinated to be scared Guard duty again in two days. He hated this shit.

Xmas In Hell

It's Christmas and it's hard to get into the holiday mood with 100 degree heat and humidity, and the constant fear of wondering if he would wake up dead one morning. They had a Christmas tree in the ward. It was sent to them by some caring veterans organization back home. His presents this year came from the head nurse who gave him a pen and pencil set and The Red Cross which gave him a "ditty bag" full of toiletries. The old woman who did his laundry and cleaned his hootch gave him a Christmas card. He didn't understand the language but he did understand the meaning. He was moved by the fact that some old woman, who he considered a lower form of life, could be so thoughtful. At midnight colored flares filled the sky and the sound of Christmas carols could be heard. He sat on his bunk and read the Christmas card over and over again. His heart filled with an intense feeling of loneliness.

It was a 12 hour work shift, seven days a week. It was a variety show for war wounds. A double amputee, bones and muscle displayed like meat in a butcher shop. He cut away blood soaked uniforms, inserted needles for fluids and held patients while a doctor struggled to insert a breathing tube. Burn patients swollen like balloons. The stench of dead skin and screams which pierced his ears. Patients with their brains scrambled or blown away. He held a femoral artery as blood gushed all over the bed. He scooped blood clots out of a guys back and tried to keep from tossing his lunch. Children with polio, TB, and leprosy. A patient went into cardiac arrest and the defibrillator didn't work and the doctor cut open the chest and massaged the heart as he fumbled to keep the patient breathing but death won. And all he remembered was the blank stare and open mouth as he placed the body in a bag and wheeled it away. They never told him it would be like this back in training.

A Village In Which Innocents Died

Anonymous village. Anonymous people. Anonymous graves.
Forgotten amid the larger consequences of war. A farmer, his head
hung low, walks through a hilltop cemetery. The Pentagon has said
little in response. Only God knows what's happened to them. Only
God cares. The morning unfolds under a warm sun. Fields terraced
like a stepladder up the slopes. Cows pull plows for planting. Children
harvest turnip leaves. In the night as they slept the bombs were
dropped on them. No enemy here, only farmers. Dead goats and sheep
lay in the rubble. A red tractor carcass scorched and mangled. Farmers
now harvest bomb fragments. Scrap metal is valuable and winter is
near.

Troops Search A Village

Troops swoop into the village in helicopters loaded with supplies. Soldiers take up positions around the village as the medics dispense bandages and aspirin. The people are happy the troops are there. They swarm the soldiers for free tubes of Chapstick. The soldiers have raided the village before. Three people are detained and one man is taken for questioning. The troops have reason to believe the enemy is present in the village. "We have good intelligence that something is going on here," said the Captain.

War Becomes Real

He was shot twice in the chest. Another soldier sew him go down and rushed to drag him to safety. He was still alive. For a couple of seconds everything was in like slow motion. He was scared but felt no pain. He didn't know what was wrong and thought he might be dead. Once you get shot at, it's war. At 17, he should be in high school not at war.

Another Village Where Innocents Died

In the moment after the planes hit the towers. DISBELIEF. On TV it was so condensed. Then the buildings came down, slowly, surely crumbling. The horror and anger. People were in there. Nothing he could do. The people had no enemy. Now the country must seek revenge. What was the point. He had lost in Vietnam and still hadn't recovered.

Home Without A Home

I travel with a heavy backpack
strapped across my shoulders,
and a plastic bag of clothes.
When you are homeless,
these are the things you carry.
And tucked away somewhere
are the memories of a war
that are still fresh.
No yellow ribbons greeted me
when I returned home.
Now I soldier on each day
trying to find some place to call my own,
riding late night buses to shelters
only to be rousted out at dawn.
A private first class,
now a second class war veteran
walking the dark streets.
Home but without a home.

American Dream

A small house.
A quiet street.
Colors balance.
Chi flows.
A childhood dream
come true.
Harmony abounds.
All seems wonderful.
Life in full bloom.
Day,
after day,
after day.

Honor

He sits on a bench
by the corner store.
His face weathered
and his clothes worn
A cart of cans next to him.
As a young man, he went to war.
Today, he sits on the street
cast aside,
like the junk
he collects.
Devoted
to duty
and service,
love of country
and respect
for it's leaders.
Has his country
served him as well,
as he served it?

The Soul Returns

The scenery looked alot like back home. The sun popped out from behind the clouds and everything looked so rural. The sheep were in a pasture along with horses and cows grazing on a green carpet of grass. The train was crowded with students headed to the west coast for holiday. In Athlone, I took a taxi to the hotel. The place seemed so familiar but I had never been there before. In search of my soul, I walked by the lake. It was cold and misty. I saw an old man who looked like my grandfather. But it couldn't be for he had died many years ago. The old man called to me and asked for directions. I couldn't help for I was a stranger in this land myself. The old man shook my hand and thanked me anyway and walked away. I had a dream in the war in which my grandfather had come to visit me and took my soul for safekeeping. Now years later in a small town in Ireland the home of my ancient ancestors my soul had been returned to me.

We entered grade school in 1954 not as friends but just classmates. I finished school but they became dropouts. Bugsey, tall, skinny, thick, black framed glasses always gave me crap for being overweight. He left school in junior high and ended up in Vietnam. Dick with his slicked black hair and cowboy boots was always picking on kids. He put a mouse in his mouth to scare the girls. Dick let school in 11th grade and ended up in Vietnam. Ernie was from the farm and smelled like manure. He always talked about sex. We made fun of him. He quit school in eight grade and later ended up in Vietnam. Tony and I were altar boys. We would sneak some communion wine and Sister Odeil would give us a hard time. Tony left school his senior year and ended up in Vietnam. Roger was just a face in the crowd. I can't remember when Roger left school but he also ended up in Vietnam.

Bugsey drives a cab at night and lives in a one room apartment. He has his share of drinking bouts and urinates on the bathroom floor and wonders why it stinks. Dick won some medals in the war. He works at night cleaning buildings. They say he did some prison time. Ernie went to Vietnam twice and came back to the farm. He started drinking and raising hell and shot himself one day while in the barn. Tony sits in his room all day and smokes cigarettes, drinks beer and watches porno movies. The voices in his head telling him he is soon to be dead. Roger came home from Vietnam just another body in a box. I ended up in Vietnam too and drank to much and nearly lost my mind but never hope. And then one day I fell in love with a woman who taught me to love myself and put the memories of shattered lives to rest.

www.ingramcontent.com/pod-product-compliance
Lightning Source LLC
Chambersburg PA
CBHW031959040426

42448CB00006B/429